Buildings that feel good

Buildings that feel good

Ziona Strelitz

RIBA Publishing

Contents

© Ziona Strelitz, 2008

Published by RIBA Publishing, 15 Bonhill Street, London EC2P 2EA

ISBN 978 1 85946 296 6

Stock Code 64211

Main cover image *Pentland Lakeside* © Morley von Sternberg www.vonsternberg.com
Montage of cover images taken from the book. For a full list of picture credits see page 147

British Library Cataloguing in Publications Data
A catalogue record for this book is available from the British Library.

Publisher: Steven Cross
Commissioning Editor: Matthew Thompson
Project Editor: Anna Walters
Designed by Alex Lazarou, Surbiton, UK
Typeset by Alex Lazarou, Surbiton, UK
Printed and bound by Cambridge University Press, Cambridge

RIBA Publishing is part of RIBA Enterprises Ltd
www.ribaenterprises.com

To the many clients, colleagues, co-judges and collaborators on project teams with whom I've worked to help envision, analyse and shape built settings over the years. To the many people who've shared their reactions as building users in fascinating, instructive and enjoyable research. And to continued learning and other exemplary buildings to follow.

Foreword

Sir Philip Dowson CBE PPRA RIBA

Architecture is unique in that it is the only art that we inhabit. The roof over our heads is our first security but what is enduring is the power that fine buildings possess to move us and to reflect the mood consonant with their purpose. Indeed, at their highest level and in the hands of a great architect, buildings can give visible shape to spiritual aspirations. For straightforward and more ordinary buildings however, whatever qualities they may aim to possess and communicate, let them firstly aim to welcome and to reassure if they are not to alienate people and so become unloved.

In Ziona Strelitz's handsome volume *Buildings that feel good*, she addresses this subject with twenty examples of a variety of building types and scale. These include large stand-alone buildings as well as schemes which address landscape and the construction of places.

The author comes with authority to her subject from the perspective of someone with a background in social anthropology, town planning, and interior design, who has for many years studied issues that face the occupiers' brief and post-occupancy results. Over these years she has collected an empirical set of research findings which she sets out as an agenda to feed and inform the process of design from concept to completion. These draw from the carefully selected projects and are illustrated and discussed with a clear and important message.

Today, we need the integration of complex technical imperatives to meet current demands for sustainable solutions. This in turn requires that we constantly have to reinterpret technology in human terms if we are to preserve a place for *value* in our world of fact, and so create buildings and places that people can relate to and enjoy and which can awaken their loyalties and with it a sense of belonging.

The author quotes Vitruvius, who, writing in the first century BC, encapsulated the basis of good architecture as 'firmness, commodity and delight' – still true as ever. The emphasis here is specifically on delight, echoing Gropius's entreaty for building-makers to 'recover a comprehensive vision of the wholeness of the environment in which we live. In our technical and mechanised society we should passionately emphasise that we are still a world of men, and man must be the focus of all planning'. In her book, the author engages splendidly – and on her own terms – with this human issue, drawing important lessons from 'buildings that feel good'.

Acknowledgements

This book could not have been written without the support of the many architects and clients whose projects form the content for the case study analyses. Much of the information was originally gathered in the course of research on good design for CABE, and all the case studies involved considerable dialogue to check facts. I greatly appreciate everyone's responsiveness in this process. The case study selection, analyses and interpretations are of course my own.

The final result benefits enormously from the support of numerous photographers who have been generous in making their work available. I particularly thank Nick Wood who has let me use his images freely over many years, and the following who have kindly provided images for the book: Chris Gascoigne, Dennis Gilbert, Mick Hurdus, Ian Lawson, Joe Miles, Marcus Robinson, Timothy Soar, Mark Tupper and Morley von Sternberg. The opportunity to select from many possible images was a challenge. Amongst the colleagues at ZZA who have played a role in this, special thanks are due to René Barownick. Every effort has been made to credit all contributors correctly – I trust that we have got that right, and whole-hearted apologies if we have not. It is no disrespect to architectural photographers that a number of ZZA's own images are used as illustrations. I am not a professional in this art, but my interests lead me to observing and capturing different things.

In conversations we have had about architecture, place and people over the years, Sir Philip Dowson has always struck a distinctive and memorable note. I very much value his lending these views in the Foreword.

The team at RIBA Publishing have played a critical part, and my thanks to them for another enjoyable collaboration, notably Matthew Thompson for his enthusiasm and staunch support, and Anna Walters for her lack of fuss in 'getting on with it'. I had not worked with the book designer, Alex Lazarou, before. He has been immensely collaborative in letting me have a say on all the spreads; I certainly hope to work with him again.

Thanks also to all those with whom I have worked on so many projects that are not referenced in this book. The insights gained have 'osmosed' into the analysis. Finally, the case studies presented are valuable and instructive, but they are not the last word. I look forward to further studies on 'More buildings that feel good'.

Ziona Strelitz

About the author

Educated as a Social Anthropologist, Town Planner and Interior Designer, in Cape Town, London and New York, Ziona Strelitz has developed a distinctive career studying people's experience of the built environment. In 1990 she founded ZZA Responsive User Environments, a research and advisory practice that helps to shape effective and sustainable buildings and settings. ZZA works with leading developers, designers and occupiers both at the briefing stage and after building occupation, mediating cultural and spatial issues to help create buildings that work for people. Ziona's perspective is enriched by her wide repertoire of professional activities: writing on people's needs and design strategies, judging building and town planning awards, and as a presenter at international conferences. Her academic involvement includes teaching on the innovative programmes in Intelligent Buildings at The University of Reading and in Interdisciplinary Design Management at The University of Hong Kong. From her base in London, Ziona continues her engagement with building users and project teams on both individual buildings and at the urban scale, in unending fascination with new data, new narratives, new design approaches, and the issues and opportunities posed by social and technological change.

EXPERIENCING GOOD DESIGN: WHAT IT FEELS LIKE

The purpose of this book is to share a series of case studies of buildings that provide good experiences for building users, and distil propositions for design. Like the truism that beautiful houses don't make happy families, and its converse, these breaks in correlation are taken as read. But buildings can do their work more and less fully. It is important to reference and understand successes and shortcomings. The focus here is on design that works well.

Giving an imprimatur of success raises inevitable questions, most obviously, success for whom? What defines them as successes? In whose opinion? With what credentials?

Many agents have roles in building production: as developers, financiers, architects, planners, engineers, surveyors, and public, corporate and private clients. With the growing tendency to building assembly – as opposed to full construction on site – component manufacturers now have a significant influence. Even brand consultants and public relations practitioners are enlisted to optimise buildings' pathway from conception to delivery and on to market acceptance. Every agent has his or her own professional perspective, with related objectives and responsibilities on a given project. To be effective, projects have to perform in all the respects that the specialists represent, not least in achieving planning consent and financial viability.

These participants all have relevant contributions to make. Hopefully at least one party on a project team has a framework for seeing the overall picture, and the skill and authority to integrate the various inputs. In any event, the process of conceiving, shaping and delivering a building involves a multitude of opportunities for influence. It also involves myriad separate design decisions that will impinge on the outcome, whether or not all these steps and their interactions are explicit and recognised.

The issue underlying this book is how these numerous inputs converge in practice, in the experience of people who use buildings.

Of course, we all use buildings
– as residents, workers, passengers and
shoppers, and in the pursuit of education,
health and cultural and sporting activities.
We also use them as elements that
structure and define the wider settings that
we inhabit and visit. They affect the nature
and identity of places.

The variety of capacities in which people
use even buildings of similar types
– as corporate directors, globe-trotting
managers, process workers occupying
their desks five days a week, and also
as the buildings' cleaners – does entail
differences of need and expectation. This
does not nullify the potential for insight on
the building users' perspective; rather it
underpins its complexity.

The realm of the building user has been
the focus of my professional work for
many years. It continues as an instructive
and evolving field of learning and design
feedback. The disciplines on which my
research and strategic design work
were established anchor it in social
anthropology, town planning and interior
design, affording an educated alertness
to social and cultural perspectives and to
the range of spatial scales at which we use
the built environment. I have conducted
systematic research on how people
use built settings, and how the many
constituent elements that define buildings,
interiors and external spaces meet
people's aspirations and requirements
– emotionally and functionally. The studies
comprising this research are based on
extensive observation and dialogue with
building users.

This professional journey first focused
on inquiry 'after the event', or what the
industry refers to as 'post-occupancy
evaluation'. The findings constitute a rich
corpus of work. The focus diversified when
clients asked: 'Where were you before we
spent the money?', requesting that the
accumulated knowledge of user reactions
be input at the early stages of project
concept and design review.

Clients and designers seek the approach
to structured engagement with users to be
applied at the front end of their projects,
to establish what users think they would
value in a future building whilst its design
remains open to influence. The specific
challenge of accessing user opinion
to inform a project's design when the
occupier or end-users are not yet known
is resolved by talking to interviewees with
reference characteristics similar to those
of the anticipated users.

The two key stages of research to inform
briefing, pre- and post-construction, are
not entirely discrete. Much of the building
industry's work occurs in building interiors,
and these are altered and replaced – often
numerous times – within a building's life.
The increasing practice of producing
buildings as 'shell and core' – that is the
building structure, envelope and basic
services – makes the differences in life
span explicit, with the building as the more
enduring container, and its fit-out more
ephemeral, and typically involving looser
elements that are procured by the building
occupier.

Some buildings are more radically
recycled, with interventions to fundamental
elements. The case studies that follow
include several such examples, as
important references to the strong and
rapidly growing interest in sustainability.
Whilst the prevalent focus of sustainability
is to reduce the energy used in conducting
our lives – including the energy required
to run buildings – it has numerous other
important facets. On the level of the
physical environment, it includes buildings'
scope to provide extended utility from
their 'embodied energy' – the energy that
is used in their production, including the
production and transport of the materials
of which they are built. Socially, buildings
have a potential role in expressing and
perpetuating cultural memory, an attribute
that may have special relevance in times of
widespread change to the building stock.

There is a further link between buildings'
conception and structured learning after
they have been built. Many client bodies
and all professional contributors undertake
multiple projects in the course of their
careers. Developing a sense of what has
worked well or otherwise for an existing
building is a powerful way to inform new
design. Having the opportunity to access
completed buildings, and especially
buildings that are in use – to study and
experience them as living outcomes of
the design and production processes
that defined them – is a valuable route to
learning.

The knowledge acquired by such inquiry
is cumulative. Cookie-cutter buildings
excepted, no set of design decisions is
ever replicated in its entirety. Sites vary,
and cultural influences evolve – within
society and organisations and hence on
people as building users. One never looks
at a building in use having 'seen it all
before'. And even if there were no other
changes, one's vantage point alters, as
one's understanding is enhanced by further
observation and inquiry.

Through my practice in brief formulation,
design evaluation and judging buildings
as candidates for awards, I have assessed
many buildings at different stages of
development and use, interviewed many,
many building users, analysed their
responses, discussed and reflected
on attributes of success as well as
shortcomings. My experience as a
systematic observer of buildings in use
and through review of iterative design
proposals has provided a repertoire of
first-hand empirical knowledge from
which to distinguish approaches that
make a positive difference. My work
with colleagues fulfilling other roles on
project teams has provided the valuable
rounded context in which to appreciate
the implications of user advocacy in the
context of other project imperatives. My
work with clients responsible for large
property portfolios has afforded structured
access to older buildings as well as to new
ones.

Having the opportunity to reference completed buildings,
especially buildings in use – to study and experience them as living
outcomes of the design and production processes that defined
them – is a valuable route to learning.

This is important in distinguishing what holds up over time, and what was a 'five-minute wonder' that may have had initial marketing impact in securing tenant interest, but has eroded in relevance since.

One of the briefing methods that I use with clients is leading visits to appropriate reference buildings, to inform their thought – on a specific building project or their overall approach. For a bespoke enquiry, the selection of reference buildings is always tailored to what the given team seeks to create. Visiting a series of buildings together – stopping, staring, analysing, discussing and reflecting on what stands out as instructive, and why – has always been helpful in setting visions and identifying possible strategies to achieve them. The qualification regarding 'possible' strategies is intentional. The manifold attributes and elements involved in any project underlie the interactions between them. The site and context are fundamental. Next is the basic building arrangement, with all the potential permutations of plan shape and size, core position and configuration, sectional height, and structure and envelope closely integral. It is at this level that the building's enduring impact is established, in its scope to make a positive difference to user experience – consistently and over the long haul, whatever short-term changes may be rung in the interior fit-out. Learning from buildings that feel good instructs us in creating buildings of lasting value, in their use both as accommodation and as elements with which we engage in the built fabric around us.

The inclusive reference to 'us' is also intentional. The scope to learn and the learning process are continuous. The more projects one can reference, the richer the knowledge on which one can draw. The relevant knowledge to inform buildings that feel good includes data on materiality, but focuses on its relation to a sense of 'feel'. It is this insight that I aim to share with colleagues when we visit buildings together. And it is this dimension of experience that is essential in the establishment of searching project visions, without which (and without their clear articulation) buildings risk offering less than they could.

Visions are the start. This book also shares know-how on design translation. Without being able to tailor the selection of case studies to readers' particular projects or vantage points (which will inevitably vary), the underlying assumption is a shared quest to create buildings of greater value. The focus adopted here is on buildings that satisfy users – buildings that feel good.

This is not to endorse every aspect of all the case studies, but to highlight things they have done well – achievements that stand out in the large repertoire of buildings I have seen or studied. It is a sufficient criterion for an exemplar to demonstrate one achievement really well, particularly if the conditions involved are often addressed less effectively.

Further, the exemplar buildings, whilst recent, have all stood some test of time. Their relevant points retain clarity as well as having continued validity. My own reference to these buildings, both as touch points in my evolving thought and to guide others, has been sustained.

The case studies cover a wide range of buildings types in support of many user needs – work, make, support, travel, learn, refresh and nourish. One could classify them by function – office, factory, infrastructure, travel, retail and so on. But the exemplars are aimed at appreciating user experience, and the language used helps to attune one's thinking accordingly. The case study selection includes buildings that are intensively used by many people and some where few people either work or visit. It includes large buildings and small, new buildings and others that have been successfully recycled. My experience is that learning from building types with which one is unfamiliar, and that serve different functions to those for which one is currently providing, is fertile ground for inspiration and instructive learning. This perspective defines the agenda. The concluding chapter distils the principles and the good practice that the exemplars offer.

Learning from buildings that feel good instructs us in creating buildings of lasting value, in their use both as accommodation and as elements with which we engage in the built fabric around us.

ABBEY MILLS PUMPING STATION

Meeting rigorous technical performance requirements with a contemporary design that complements the site's fine heritage buildings, and demonstrating a commitment to quality even though only one person ever works in the building and few can visit the site

Abbey Mills Pumping Station is a contemporary addition to a group of listed Victorian buildings. Public access to the site is not permitted, and very few people are employed there. The building nevertheless honours the distinguished neighbouring buildings, with an approach appropriate to its era. The result exemplifies both the positive results that can be attained with design quality as a clear objective, and the aim's undiminished relevance despite the limited presence of people in the setting.

The brief

The Abbey Mills Pumping Station, developed to renew part of London's sewerage system, lifts sewage arriving in pipes from two low-lying London catchment areas to join the gravity flows from the higher areas of north London before passing to Beckton Treatment Sewage Works in the Northern Outfall Sewer. The station reflects industry trends away from plants with a heavy staff presence and in situ maintenance, in favour of a modular approach with multiple parallel pumps that can be swapped over and replaced by spare units. With a regime involving maintenance crews coming to the site and defects remedied remotely, only one person is usually on duty at the station.

The project is heavily engineering based. As the lowest capital and energy costs involved a layout with submersible pumps, most of the plant was installed below ground. Given this and the low staff presence to operate the plant, the need for a building was indeed questioned. However, it has a role in housing the switchgear, generators and significant craneage that handle the pumps, and the cost of covering this equipment was relatively low in the context of the overall project budget.

The building lies within the curtilage of Listed Buildings and in a Conservation Area, on a site selected in the 1860s as part of Joseph Bazalgette's drainage scheme for London. Its beautiful examples of Victorian industrial architecture include two Grade 2 Listed pumping buildings – fine gothic-style structures of honey-coloured brick with decorative terracotta insets and stone carvings. The brief for Abbey Mills Pumping Station sought fine architecture again, but contemporary in design and with its primary function to support the infrastructure without determining or constraining the station's technical performance.

← Majestic scale, with luminous uplight at the top of the pumping station's large volume

Overview

Most of the station is underground, where incoming culverts pump sewage for discharge at a higher level. Above ground, the building forms a single space – 29 m wide, 57 m long and 23 m high – within which the structure is clearly legible. This is a steel framework of A-frames with stiffened column bases, and with the perimeter columns switching to curving steel rafters braced by diagonal tie-rods above eaves level. The envelope it supports is constructed almost entirely in aluminium, a material selected for its light weight and durability in the pumping station's moist environment.

The building's side and end walls are clad in aluminium panels and secure screens with aluminium louvers, allowing for the ventilation that is needed at the lower level. Four large circular terminals and four gleaming chimneys that protrude from the roof facilitate the necessary intake to and exhaust from the generators that is required at roof level. A raised clerestory with louvers at the apex of the roof provides internal ventilation. The aluminium roof has a protective zinc coating, and the wall and louver panels are coated externally in metallic spray paint (pvf2).

Inside the building, the aluminium wall, roof cladding and pipe work are all exposed – with only the high- and low-voltage switchgear in separate rooms, and a small high-level control room for local operation. Steel portal frames, at 6 m centres along the side aisles, support high-level ventilation and gallery catwalks that give ready access around the elevated areas. Access is provided to all the pumping chambers. A loading dock at the western end facilitates vehicular maintenance access to remove and return pumps and other parts of plant.

The particular lesson of Abbey Mills Pumping Station is the commitment to design of a high aesthetic standard, even though only one person works in this building. This is a touch point for those who develop buildings anywhere, particularly in highly visible settings.

↑   Articulated exterior, with bold circular terminals and delicate texture of the louvered walls

↗   The pumping station's contemporary expression, complementing the heritage neighbouring buildings (to the left)

↗↗   Long section, showing the plant's significant extent below ground level

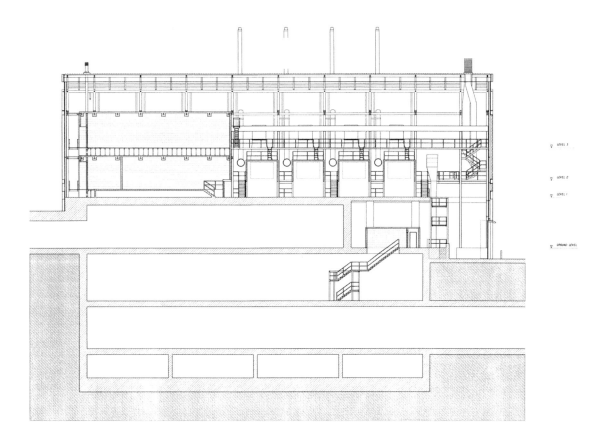

What the Abbey Mills Pumping Station shows

Aesthetic commitment

The particular lesson of Abbey Mills Pumping Station is the commitment to design of a high aesthetic standard, even though only one person works in this building. This is a touch point for those who develop buildings anywhere, and particularly in highly visible settings. Fortunately the pumping station can be seen – from local roads, a footpath close to the site, the District Line and overland trains across Abbey Creek. As part of the project, the existing Longwall Path was realigned with the top of the new delivery channels, enabling easier access for wheel- and pushchairs, and giving more extensive views over Abbey Creek and into the pumping station site. Whilst the project exemplifies good design for its own sake, this access offers some welcome scope for the resultant achievement to be viewed and enjoyed more widely.

Contemporary response

A key aspect of the aesthetic brief was the requirement for modernity. This was also championed by the local planning authority as a participant in the client-led architectural competition. A building like those already on the site would have been neither feasible nor appropriate now. Instead of mimicking them with pastiche, Abbey Mills Pumping Station is a solution of its own age. The design shows a contemporary approach in harmony with its neighbouring heritage buildings.

Materials and finish

Externally, the roof profile echoes the gothic style of the earlier buildings, but in contrast to its predecessors' brick elevations, the aluminium cladding speaks for its time. Its strength, lightness and resistance to corrosion offer functional relevance, and its versatility has enabled the rainscreen cladding to be moulded into complex shapes for the external elevations, the cylindrical cowlings and the flue farings.

Whilst the building outline is bold and clear from a more distant view, the subtle texture of the cladding suggests delicacy. The sides of the building, designed to meet the twin requirements of openness for ventilation with a security grille, provide visual texture. A subtle layering is created by the louvers' placement in front of the security screen, softening the building's appearance.

Articulating meaning

With their strong form, the cylinders and chimneys are powerful elements in the building's architectural identity. These strident elements gleam with solidity in contrast to the building's textured walls. As well as their aesthetic role in complementing the curved profile of the arched roof, their articulation of function gives meaning to the volume below.

Spatial wonder

Internally, the building is awesome. The scale of the single expanse enclosed by the superstructure is majestic. Despite the extensive equipment, the space feels coherent and legible. Different colours delineate the various systems – structure, craneage, circulation and pumps, and the stairways, catwalks and cross-bridges facilitate high-level access.

The aluminium cladding for the walls and roof is exposed inside the building. As well as its technical attributes, this has aesthetic benefits. Its silvery appearance reflects both the uplighting on the long internal elevations and the sunlight coming through the louvers in the central clerestory along the apex of the roof and through the apertures between the open louvers and security grilles. The diverse quality of light from these sources is magical. So is its interplay with the large elements of structure and plant, as pools of illumination alternate with dramatic shadows that ebb away where the reach of the light source falls off.

Technical, visual and spatial performance

This project benefited from a constructive definition of aims – for the building to match its distinguished predecessors in functionality and aesthetic standard, but not in style. Abbey Mills Pumping Station is a fine response. It exemplifies the scope to create rich spatial experience and visual refinement in a project primarily geared to a technical agenda. This need not be onerous in terms of cost; indeed, the estimate for Abbey Mills Pumping Station was reduced with successive iterations to improve the design.

↗ Short section, showing the building's memorable arched profile above ground level, and the submersed pumps below grade

→ Plans, from lowest to highest level clockwise from top left

↗↗ View at ground level, showing the scale of the pumping equipment and the rich quality of light

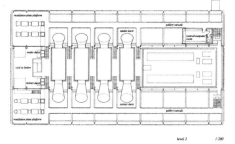

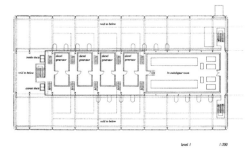

ARCHITECTS
Allies and Morrison

CLIENT
Thames Water Utilities Ltd

PROJECT ADDRESS
Abbey Mills Pumping Station
Gay Road
off Abbey Lane
Stratford
London E15 2RW

AWARDS
Aluminium Award, 1997 –
 Commendation
British Construction Industry Award,
 1997 – Commendation
RIBA Regional Award, 1997

CAFÉ IN THE SQUARE, BRINDLEYPLACE

A finely finished small sculptural building, offering a strong visual and social focus to the surrounding development

The building demonstrates the high positive impact that a single, distinctive building can make in animating a large development and enlivening a place. This influence derives from the building's flair, and the contrast of its form with its surroundings. The relatively high cost for the area it encloses is more than warranted by the signature and identity it lends to the overall development.

The brief
As a small building with a distinctive form, the café's role is to serve as the focal point for the whole of Brindleyplace, a development comprising a varied mix of uses, notably offices. The client and landscape designer envisaged a sculptural element as the main vertical feature in the new central square. The design commission for the café was inspired by the architect's iconic public WC in Westbourne Terrace. The vision for the Brindleyplace café was for a transparent, light building as a centrepiece forming the visual and social heart of the square. As the only central building in this setting, its challenge was to address both the space in which it sits and the buildings that enclose the square with conviction.

↖ The café fulfilling its key roles as a building that performs in the round, defining the square as a social setting, and integrating the arrangement of office buildings that surround it

→ Clear registration of the café building's strong form against the much larger buildings that form its backdrop

Overview

The café is a small building with significant impact. Its footprint is 14 m by 7.6 m at its widest point. The building's presence derives in part from its size, in part from its site where a radial arrangement of York stone paviours converge, and largely from its distinctive form – the eye-shaped plan and butterfly roof. The structure is a series of portal frames made from 114.3 mm diameter tubular steel sections. The vertical structural columns are continuous with the roof members. They cross over at the ridge of the roof pitch to form the canopies that resemble butterfly wings. The wings give the building added height, whilst their profile reinforces the building's footprint. The structure is braced by two horizontal tapering ovoid frames.

The frame is completely glazed – the roof and walls comprise double-glazed panels with the walls of the customer-facing area in clear glass. The roof has white dotted fritting on the outer pane to provide protection from glare and solar gain. The canopies, made from single-glazed 12 mm toughened glass, have a similar white fritting. The envelope comprises 143 glass panels involving 32 different templates. Extruded aluminium sections were made to secure the glazing and incorporate weather seals around the plate-glass doors.

To maximise the building's transparency, secure storage is provided in a basement that is accessed from an external trapdoor. The food preparation area and the WCs are obscured from internal view by their location behind the rear partition to the bar area, and from external view by fritting with a solid white enamel screenprint on the external wall.

A notable success is the comfortable environment inside the café – in both summer and winter – for what is effectively a 'greenhouse'. The 12 mm toughened single-glazed fold-back doors are hinged to open 180° against the adjacent wall. In addition, external air is pumped in mechanically overhead for summer cooling.

For winter warming, heated air is pumped in from external vents that appear as stone 'toadstools' in the grassed areas of the square and supplemented by underfloor heating. Separate supply to, and extract from, the kitchen area uses the sculpted stone vents in the adjacent grassed area, with ducting routed out through a louvered funnel.

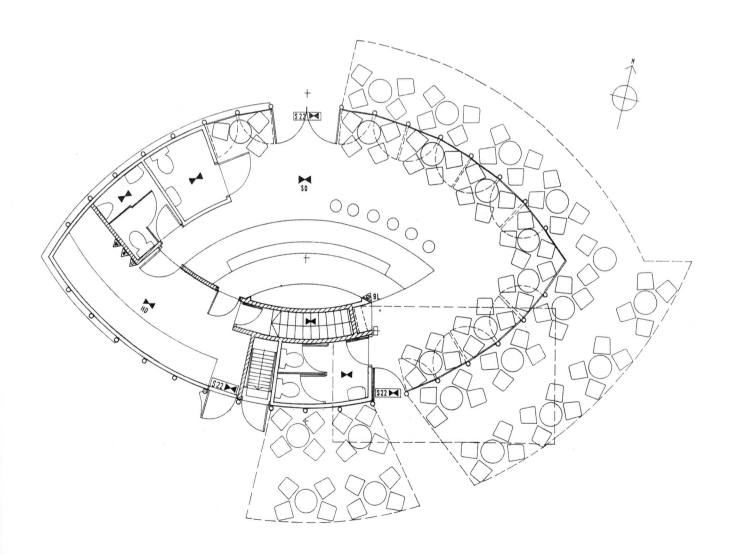

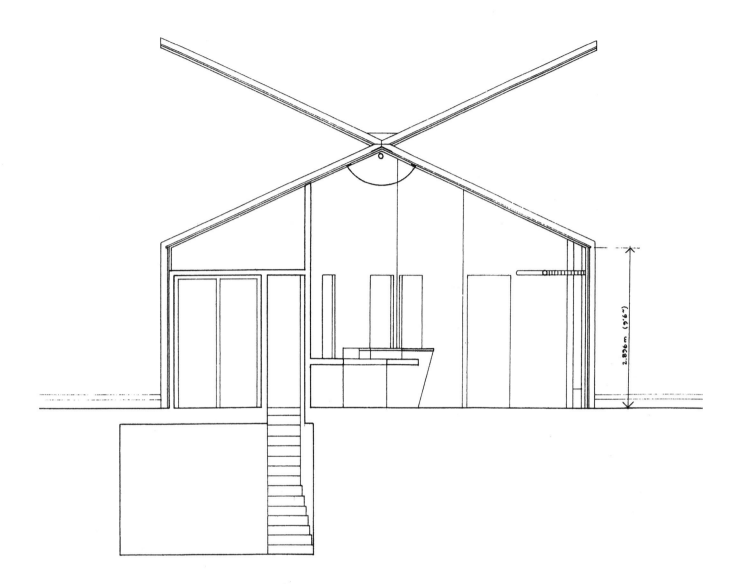

2.856m (9'6")

This is a situation where a building's role as a sculptural piece or 'object in space' is valid ... the building succeeds in unifying the surrounding structures and integrating them with the square.

↑ Short section, showing the geometry of the café's signature butterfly roof, and the catering storage below ground level

← Ground floor plan, showing scope to interface with the external setting by spilling out of the building

What the Café in the Square shows

Sculptural form, social impact

The building fulfils the brief's intentions by acting as a compelling visual focus, even in dull and wet weather. Its social purpose is also well achieved. Seating 40 people inside, and over one hundred within its precinct, the café has proved a popular venue. Its intensive use is not a case of 'needs must'; Brindleyplace has a rich range of leisure amenities and refreshment venues.

The appeal is down to good design. As the only building in a large space, it has to address its context authoritatively. As a small building, the challenge is heightened. The respective areas are significant in their contrast, with the café just 50 sq m internally and the square in which it sits some 3,800 sq m!

Whilst the café's immediate setting is the open space of the square, the square itself is contained. The elevations of the surrounding buildings provide a defined and fairly continuous edge, with some elements – rising to 48 m – taller than the prevailing six-storey height. The surrounding elevations form a rhythmic backdrop for the café, against which it stands out as a curvaceous form. This is a situation where a building's role as a sculptural piece or 'object in space' is valid. The brief envisaged the café as a vertical element with this effect, and the resultant building succeeds in unifying the surrounding structures and integrating them with the square. The café's sculptural form – defined by its ovoid plan and butterfly wing extensions to the roof glazing – is finely judged, enabling it to stand up to its orthogonal neighbours. Its distinctive form conveys its contrast of function from the surrounding offices, and evokes playful verve and joy.

↖ An effective focus in all weather: café's long elevation (top image); serving as a beacon from a pedestrian access route (lower image)

↗ Positive impact beyond the building itself: stimulating and supporting café life in its setting

Quality of detailing

These descriptions are apt. Whereas 'fun' has become shorthand for condescension and cheapness, these are far from the café's sense of command. Its visual authority derives from its form and its quality of detailing. Tube sizes are minimal and consistent, and the tubes are set at a consistent distance from one another, although some parts of the frame carry greater loads than others. The junctions are all factory welded. Because the building tapers, the glass panels vary both in size and in the angles at which they are fixed to their supporting posts. The detailing of the canopies is apparently seamless, with the outer layer of double-glazing extending over the silicone join of the units at the eaves for protection.

User comfort

The interior is also effective. A risk in setting out to design a building as an object in its setting is overlooking its requirement to accommodate people. For a patron inside this building, however, its use is both comfortable and stimulating. The management of thermal conditions, light and views has been well addressed with user comfort in mind. On sunny days, customers are protected from excessive brightness by the fritting on the upper glass panels. Internally the building provides thermal enclosure as well as visual connection to life in the square. The staff who run the facilities are also building users, and they too enjoy these benefits, although their working area is necessarily constrained.

Durable design

The Café in the Square exemplifies how a well-designed building can withstand alterations to the interior. A change in proprietorship resulted in changes to the corporate livery and replacement of the original zinc bar. Such is operational life, which durable design should be able to sustain. That the Café in the Square can accommodate such adaptations, despite being a transparent building, is a further testament to its coherence.

Small and valuable

At £7,000 per sq m in 1997, this was a very expensive building to deliver. However, as a small inhabited sculpture that creates a memorable sense of place in its setting, and accommodates pleasing functional activity inside, it offers good value on multiple fronts. Its success hinges on its quality, form and scale. Miniatures have a distinctive appeal because they can be seen in the round. The Café in the Square at Brindleyplace is a worthy 'folly'.

Its success hinges on its quality, form and scale. Miniatures have a distinctive appeal because they can be seen in the round. The Café in the Square at Brindleyplace is a worthy 'folly'.

ARCHITECTS
CZWG Architects LLP

CLIENT
Argent plc

PROJECT ADDRESS
The Café in the Square
Main Square
Brindleyplace
Birmingham B1 2HL

AWARDS
BIAT Open Award for Technical
    Excellence, 1997 – Commendation
Civic Trust Award, 1998 – Outstanding
    Scheme, Birmingham
Royal Fine Art Commission / BSkyB
    Building of the Year Award, 1998
    – Small Buildings category

CHISWICK PARK

A series of office buildings providing efficient space and fine internal quality, with an innovative masterplan that affords intensive use of the site and a large central landscaped oasis

Chiswick Park is exemplary in terms of masterplanning and architecture. The site is organised in a pod format, with all vehicular traffic routed around the perimeter, creating a large pedestrian area at the heart of the development. The buildings are arranged inside the perimeter route, addressing this focal landscaped space. Architecturally, they are variations on a generic model that offers good views and light to individuals, floor plates that can be harnessed for a wide variety of internal plans, and effective lettable area for the landlord. The buildings' spatial attributes derive from the interplay of core design, floor-plate depth, sectional height and perimeter glazing. External shading mitigates internal solar gain. The external brise-soleils and fire stairs contribute to the buildings' technical performance. As key elements in a consistent design vocabulary that gives the development its strong visual coherence, these features also contribute to Chiswick Park's identity.

The brief
Chiswick Park has been developed on a former bus works opposite Gunnersbury Station. A previous scheme for the 133,550 sq m site in the late 1980s was based on a central vehicular approach, and a variety of office buildings with different stylistic identities, designed by a range of architects. That scheme was halted after the start of infrastructure work and foundations. The succeeding concept for the park, as now substantially built, is in sharp contrast.

Chiswick Park is distinct in its focus on people. It is masterplanned for pedestrians' enjoyment, with vehicular movement routed behind the buildings and the central area conserved as a landscaped open space for communal use. Another objective, for the park to be part of the local realm, is fulfilled in its provision of open access to local people. A related aim underpins Chiswick Park's concept, 'Enjoy-work', with the mix of uses that complement its predominant office function.

A further focus is environmental sustainability. One aspect is access. Parking provision is geared to 75 per cent of the site population walking or cycling to work or arriving by public transport. Other key aspects are intensive site use, and building design that offers extensive external aspect, with integrated passive provision to reduce solar gain. The developer's interest in lean construction is reflected in the significant use of pre-fabricated elements, an approach that facilitates cost-effective incorporation of high-quality detailing.

↖ One of the endless fine views on site, all offering a rich interplay between architecture and landscape

Overview

The central water feature at Chiswick Park, on axis with the entrance, is on two levels, connected by a 1.8 m high waterfall and bordered by soft landscaping and timber boardwalks. The buildings are arranged on either side of this, facing one another and fronted by pedestrian paths. Deeper into the site, to the west of the lake, are three buildings arranged around a hard-landscaped plaza that serves as an events arena and pitch for sports activities, further increasing the amenity area and sense of open space.

The buildings that address one another across the central axis are four storeys high, with some taller buildings deeper into the site. The masterplan allows for 12 buildings, providing an eventual 139,354 sq m gross of office space and ancillary uses, including leisure and retail facilities.

Stability is provided by the post-tensioned flat concrete slabs, supported on pre-cast columns and edge beams using a 9 m by 9 m structural grid tied back to a central steel frame core.

This technique reflects the developer's concern to maximise construction efficiency and minimise the use of raw materials. The preference for off-site pre-fabrication is seen in the specification of the pre-cast concrete, the curtain walling – a unitised system using 3 m by 4 m glazed panels – and the air-handling plant.

Internally, the buildings provide large floor areas of 18 m depth between central core and full perimeter glazing, with 3 m clear height from floor to ceiling.

The energy strategy, which facilitates low running costs, involves a displacement ventilation system to provide comfort cooling, and extensive use of outside air for cooling without additional refrigeration for a large part of the year. There are fixed external sunshades or brise-soleils and active fabric blinds to minimise solar gain. Car-parking space is at ground level to the rear of the buildings – screened by hedges, and in undercroft areas below the buildings, accessed from the perimeter service road. These areas are neither open to, nor visible from, the front elevations.

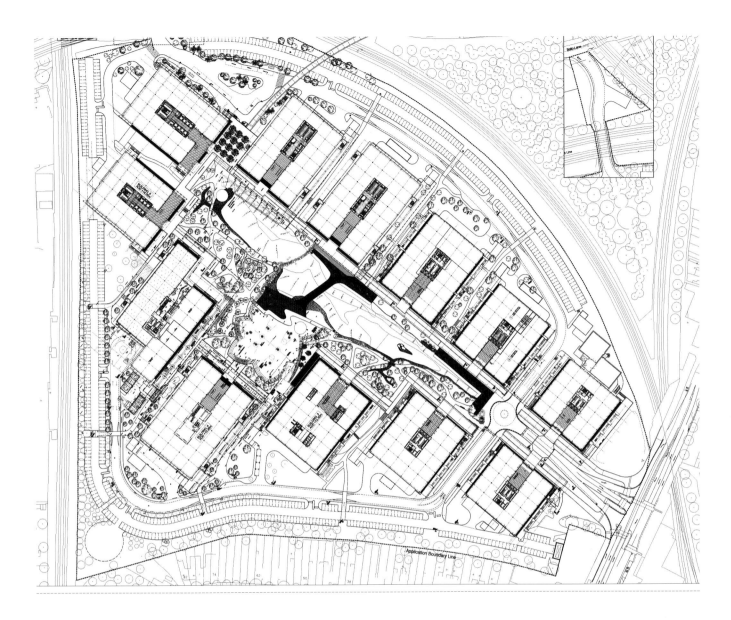

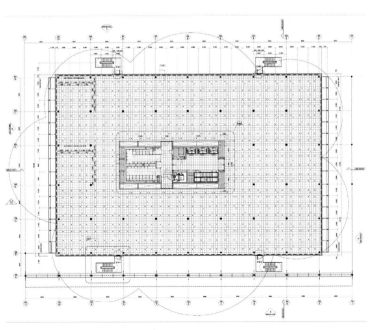

← Wide variety of user experience in the central and soft landscaped space

↑ Masterplan, showing the highly efficient arrangement of buildings that optimises use of the site, the perimeter vehicular access route, and the critical mass of amenity space in the central pedestrian area

→ Typical floor plan, showing core arrangement that facilitates unimpeded space, good natural light and clear views across and out from the floor plate

What Chiswick Park shows

Beneficial masterplan

Chiswick Park offers valuable precepts for sustainability, in both its masterplan and buildings. Shortly after entering the site, all vehicular movement is routed behind the buildings. Implicit in this strategy is the important decision not to provide vehicular access including passenger drop-off at the front of the buildings. This has generated an environment that is people focused, user-friendly and safe. Dedicating the open space at the heart of the site as a pedestrian preserve affords an unusually high degree of visual amenity as well as uninterrupted functional use as relaxation space. The high standard of the landscaping and site maintenance add to users' enjoyment.

Integration with community

The next key decision was not to gate the development. Chiswick Park is not only for those who work there, but also for local people who use its facilities such as the bar, restaurant, gym and landscaped area, with its central lake, bridge, boardwalks, grass areas and semi-mature trees. The entrance to Chiswick Park is not cordoned. Seeing people with young children stroll along the boardwalk during the working day is a practical demonstration that new workplace developments can be integrated with the local urban realm, even where they are privately owned and managed.

Work as part of life

The scheme's mix of facilities contributes to the locality, increasing the range of local uses that includes a well-established high street. Chiswick Park's location close to residential settings enables people to live close to their workplace, promoting scope for employment without the inevitable requirement of onerous travel to work. These characteristics support work-life balance and help in making Chiswick Park and its local context socially sustainable places.

External detailing and identity

The buildings are distinct on several counts. One is the focus on pre-fabrication, enabling high-quality to be achieved quickly and cost-effectively. Once the key components of the design are manufactured and perfected, the unit cost involved in their wide use across the development is reduced with each application. This underlies the replication of features from building to building. The approach has resulted in prominent and distinctively detailed external design features – notably the castings in the external steel frames that support the fixed brise-soleils and the external metal fire stairs down the side elevations. Another benefit is the high level of stylistic and visual unity based on the signature aesthetic. This plays a powerful role in defining Chiswick Park, and – with the consistent building scale – lending a strong sense of architectural order.

Internal spatial quality

The buildings' interior spatial quality is of strong relevance to their users. The organisations occupying the space have the benefit of large clear floor plates that they can deploy for a variety of internal plans. This flexibility is demonstrated by the range of businesses that have selected these buildings as the base for their operations – from short-term serviced office use with a predominantly cellular fit-out, through intensive call-centre activity in the open plan, to research and marketing activity in lower-density open plan, and media businesses with specialist facilities for television production and transmission. Another advantage of the masterplan is its scope for technical studios to be incorporated behind individual buildings, without compromising the visual rhythm in the central area.

Chiswick Park offers the combined benefits of deeper floor plates that are effective for organisations, and the high standard of internal spatial quality that matters to building users. This is achieved in several ways, notably through the generous height from floor to ceiling and the full-height continuous perimeter glazing. Together these design features maximise the views out from the buildings and the perceived natural light inside them – even from the deepest parts of the floor plate by the central core.

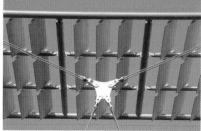

The focus on pre-fabrication, enabling high-quality to be achieved quickly and cost-effectively has resulted in prominent and distinctively detailed external design features – notably the castings in the external steel frames that support the fixed brise-soleils and the external fire stairs down the side elevations.

← High quality detailing contributing to the visual vocabulary of Chiswick Park: castings and louvers

↗ Fine internal spatial quality provided by the base building, enabling excellent daylight and external views across the floor plate

Chiswick Park demonstrates important pathways to sustainable planning and design. The benefits are numerous – to the locality, the occupier organisations, the building users and the developer.

This light and airy internal feel that users welcome is further promoted by externalising the fire stairs, with the associated advantage of eliminating visual obstruction on the floor plates. In addition, the brise-soleils play a role in evening up the perceived lighting levels across the floor plate, helping to optimise conditions wherever individuals are on the floor.

The key to the successful achievement of spatial quality in combination with deep space and responsible environmental performance is the integrated design approach.

The solutions to reducing solar gain – in spite of the extensive glazing that affords the high level of user amenity – include the brise-soleils on the south elevations and the active external fabric shades, operated from a roof-mounted weather station, on the east and west elevations.

Sustainability pays
Chiswick Park demonstrates important pathways to sustainable planning and design. The benefits are numerous – to the locality, the occupier organisations and the building users. The vision that has delivered these benefits is the developer's.

They benefit too, both from efficient use of the site – which is 50 per cent more densely developed than a typical business park, despite its large open area – and from the high ratio of productive space in the buildings, with their net to gross efficiency of up to 92 per cent on a typical floor. The developers' interests in 'buildability' – minimising wastage and improving construction speed, safety and quality of the finished buildings – have generated further benefits to both the users and themselves.

ARCHITECTS
Rogers Stirk Harbour + Partners

CLIENT
Stanhope plc

PROJECT ADDRESS
Chiswick Park
566 Chiswick High Road
London W4 5YA

AWARDS
BCO Award, 2002 – Best of the Best
BCO Award, 2002 – Best Commercial
    Workplace, London (within M25)
BCO Award, 2002 – Best Commercial
    Workplace, National
Civic Trust Award, 2002

CITIGROUP CENTRE

This tall building with an offset core demonstrates both the pivotal role that spatial organisation can play in animating a building and the strong complementary contribution by materials and integrated artwork

The building has a distinctive arrangement, with its service core at one end of a full-height atrium. Users cross the void via a series of bridges to the floor plates on the opposing block. The configuration optimises the quality of the workspace and facilitates extensive external views from the main floor plates as well as through the atrium's north and south elevations. It also generates dramatic views inside the atrium. The bridges' integral role in the building's horizontal circulation ensures the atrium's animation in the course of the building's use. The choice of materials, finishes and a large-scale commissioned sculpture extending down most of the volume's height further enliven the space.

The brief

Seeking to amalgamate its Central London offices in the late 1990s, Citigroup (formerly Citibank) opted for a new purpose-built headquarters building at Canary Wharf. The bank required 60,000 sq m of office accommodation with large spans of space, including two open floor plates for use as trading floors. The resultant 18-storey building is one of a cluster of tall buildings that have been developed in the Canary Wharf financial district since the early 1990s.

The design needed to respond to requirements governing building heights that were established as part of the original Masterplan Agreement for the Canary Wharf Development. Based on this, the parcel to the east of the site could be developed to a height of some 200 m. There was also the opportunity to extend the site and incorporate the space between the building's eastern boundary and the western boundary of the next building plot to the east. In the event, Citigroup subsequently commissioned a second, more conventional tower building on this adjoining eastern site, and this now abuts the east elevation of the case study building, with internal links between the two.

← Rich atrium experience, enlivened by extensive external views, the movement of people passing from the lift core to the building's operational floors, reflections in the surface materials and the colourful artwork down most of the volume's height

→ Exterior, showing the core tower linked to the main accomodation tower by the full height atrium with its structural cross-bracing

Overview

The building comprises 96,000 sq m of gross internal area, with 60,120 sq m net, including two 3,000 sq m trading floors and ancillary facilities to support corporate and investment banking activities.

The space is arranged in three distinct parts. The main accommodation block to the west rises 17 floors above ground floor level. A taller service core to the east, rising the equivalent of 25 storeys, contains the lifts, WCs, building services and meeting rooms, as well as building plant on its upper floors. The two blocks are linked by an atrium that extends to the full height of the western block. A massive coloured sculpture by Bridget Riley hangs down the atrium's eastern edge.

The building is oriented westwards, with the glazed western block accommodating most of the office space, the trading floors, a staff restaurant, auditorium, health centre and gym.

Its top two floors accommodate senior executive offices, client facilities and executive dining rooms that open onto a roof terrace with panoramic views of London. The four floors below ground level contain car parking and support facilities for information technology.

Secondary atria, commencing at levels 6, 9 and 12, step back from the atrium into the floor plate of the western block. These enable natural light to reach the office zones furthest from the glazing on the external elevations. They also create internal patio areas that overlook and are viewed from the main atrium, and can be accessed from the office space on their respective levels.

The opaquely clad eastern services tower contains two banks of six glass lifts, the escape stairs, the WCs, and mechanical and electrical services. All the building's vertical circulation above the second floor is located here. At street level, the building is accessed via granite-paved entrances at the atrium base to the north and south, with direct access by escalator from the Jubilee Line Station below.

The structural system comprises concrete basement and cores, steel superstructure and composite floors. Externally, the structural frame is articulated with silver-anodised aluminium panels on every three floors. These relate to structural cross-braces that connect the east and west towers. The office façades of the western tower are fully glazed with high-performance, unitised triple-skin panels that wrap around the building's curved corners. The glazing system returns into the building to clad the internal atrium, in this case as a single-glazed system. The eastern tower is clad with gunmetal-grey aluminium rain screen panels that are also used internally.

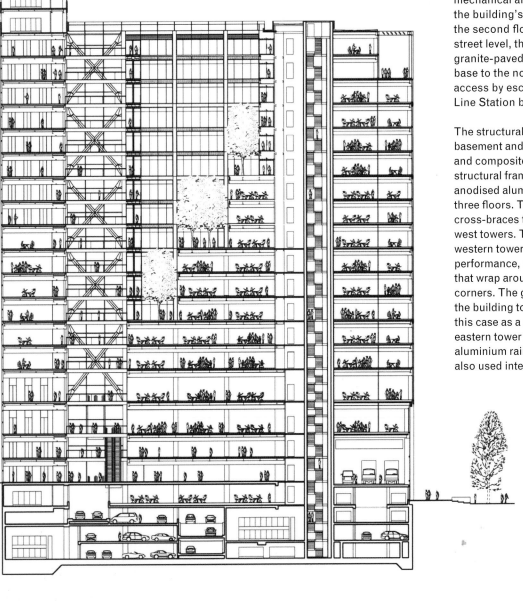

What the Citigroup building shows

Benefits of offset core

The Citigroup building is defined by its plan that isolates the building services within a dedicated block, liberating the office space from the impact of the major core functions. This allows for unobstructed space of high quality in the office block. These floor plates offer flexibility for internal planning by the occupier, and give users good access to external views on the three external elevations – encompassing the panorama of Canary Wharf, the Thames, the City and London's West End. This strategy dispenses with the need for the roof to accommodate cooling towers and other mechanical equipment, enabling the top floor of the office block to be used for accommodation.

Each of the two trading floors accommodates 500 traders and intensive use of information technology – in many cases involving rows of monitors at individual workstations. The office floors have a typical clear floor-to-ceiling height of 2.7 m, whereas a floor-to-ceiling height of 3.95 m on the large trading floors promotes a sense of spaciousness and user comfort. Uplighting the ceiling plane brightens the extensive surface above the big trader spaces.

All circulation from the lift lobbies to the working areas traverses or edges the atrium void. The link bridges on every level from 2 to 17 – and below this, the escalators between the lower-ground and second level – make the atrium completely integral to, and an active part of, the building. It works as a functional hub.

Atrium animation

The atrium is key to users' experience of the building. Its essential role for horizontal circulation ensures its animation from people's movement. Every journey along the atrium edge and across the bridges creates a visual narrative. Other sources of dynamic interest are the reflections of people, the sculpture and the lighting in the polished black granite floors and ceilings of the atrium bridges and perimeter routes.

Views, external and internal

A rigorously designed space, the atrium provides rich views both externally and within. The continuous glazing affords contrasting northward and southward views out at all levels. The key routes that one must cross to move between the lift landings, WCs and the workspace also ensure one's engagement with external views.

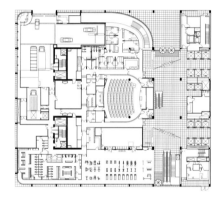

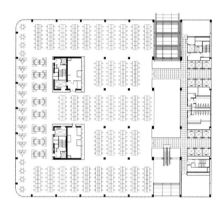

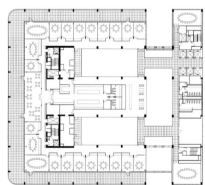

← East-west section, showing the internal arrangement with the offset core east of the full-height atrium, and the graduation in size of the floor plates, corresponding with the sub-atria introduced up the height of the building

↗ Varied floor plates: ground floor (top left then clockwise), trading floor adjacent to the main atrium on level 2, and incremental introduction of sub-atria on the 8th and 15th floors

Internally, there is a rich field of vertical, diagonal and horizontal vistas – to different levels, across the secondary atria, and through the internal elevations. This promotes interest as well as legibility, with users able to make visual connections from all points to the building as a whole and to different parts of the organisation. There is a risk with this degree of visual permeability; the architecture entrusts the vista of the office space to the custodianship of the occupier, and the uses that are allocated to the internal perimeter zone of the floor plate assume significance in defining the view.

Integrated artwork

The atrium's role as the heart of the Citigroup building is accentuated by the vast hanging sculpture by the artist Bridget Riley, suspended over 16 floors across the inner atrium elevation of the eastern tower. The commissioning of this significant artwork is integral to the building's architecture and to users' experience of the building. With its bright palette that contrasts with the atrium's muted colours, this lively textured plane is seen from the office areas and every vantage point in the atrium, including the essential circulation routes. The gentle movement of its aluminium parallelograms and their alteration in appearance with variations in light contribute further to a dynamic experience of the space. Their positions relative to one another also vary, as do the views through the spaces between them, as one moves up, across and around the atrium.

Cross-bracing and bridges

The prominent cross-bracing, external to the atrium's glazed elevation to the north and internal on the south, is another strong feature, signifying the building on the exterior as well as within. This structure 'contains' the lofty volume. It gives users a sense of assurance and robustness that balances the seemingly infinite outward views that are exposed by the high degree of visual permeability at every level.

The design of the bridges is another success, with their generous width – 3.6 m – and their 1.65 m vertical glazed edges mitigating a sense of insecurity that users often feel when traversing a narrow strip over a high void.

→ Atrium base enlivened by activity and purpose: building entrance and reception

↗ Key features that enrich the atrium experience: external views, people's movement around and across the space, and changing relationships to the suspended artwork

↗↗ Doubling the atrium's vitality: the effect of the reflective surfaces in generating visual interest

Internally, there is a rich field of vertical, diagonal and horizontal vistas – to different levels, across the secondary atria, and through the internal elevations. This promotes interest as well as legibility, with users able to make visual connections from all points to the building as a whole and to different parts of the organisation.

Calm setting, stimulating place
The atrium provides a distinctive spatial experience, but not without challenges. One is the lower ratio of lettable space than would have been achieved with a more typical approach to rental efficiency. Another is the fire strategy, which was innovatively resolved.

The atrium's conception and execution has resulted in a unique place that extends vertically through the building. It binds the building's parts and generates a visible pulse both from the sources of movement within it and the rhythmic repetition of elements up and down its elevation.

The dynamic effects are the more stimulating, given that the atrium itself is a calm setting, with a restrained palette and rigorous quality of finishes and detailing.

ARCHITECTS
Foster and Partners

CLIENT
Citibank and Canary Wharf
Contractors Ltd

PROJECT ADDRESS
1 Canada Square
Canary Wharf
London E14 5AD

AWARDS
BCO Award, 2001
 National Corporate Workplace
BCO Award, 2001
 South and East of England Regional
 Corporate Workplace

CITY OF MANCHESTER STADIUM

The stadium combines provision for high standards of viewing, user comfort and crowd safety, with an elegant sweeping structure that exerts strong visual appeal and contributes to 'place-making' inside and out

The project exemplifies the rounded benefits that can be obtained from an ambitious definition of performance requirements – for individual users and spectators as a crowd, for players and patrons, and for people in the local setting. The building sets a high standard for ease of operation. Its powerful visual impact confers prestige on the club and the city, and contributes both to the stadium's role in local urban regeneration and its scope to sustain this. The City of Manchester Stadium also demonstrates the potential to design for flexibility through a staged process of construction, enabling use for distinct sequential events, each requiring a significantly different capacity and configuration.

The brief

The stadium resulted from a series of competitive bids – first for the 2000 Olympics, next for a national stadium, before succeeding for the Queen's Golden Jubilee Commonwealth Games. In support of the objective for sustained regeneration through assured use, Manchester City Football Club became tenants after the Games, with an agreement to generate wider benefits by making the stadium available for 100 days of community use a year.

The consecutive requirements for the stadium commenced with 41,000 spectators at an athletics event in 2002, extending the next year to accommodate 48,000 spectators for football, as well as alternative use as a concert venue with combined stand and pitch capacity for 50–60,000 people.

The brief was for a high-profile venue to reflect Manchester as a major sporting centre. The all-round experience for users was to be excellent – from convenient, safe entry and exit, through to fine viewing conditions, in a breathtaking atmosphere, with a calm ambience at half-time. In terms of value, all the elements were aimed at fulfilling multiple functions, with a design that offered clarity. To ensure vibrant activity in its local setting on non-match days, the stadium was conceived as being set in a mixed-use development.

← Exhilarating arcs and fine viewing conditions benefiting from daylighting at the rear of the stand and the front edge of the stadium roof

Overview

The City of Manchester Stadium is at the heart of the new Sportcity development on a brownfield site in Eastfields, 1.5 km east of the city centre. The pre-cast concrete stadium bowl provides a gross internal area of 69,000 sq m, with a building footprint of 31,790 sq m and overall dimensions of 230 m by 260 m. The stadium is 33 m high on the east and west stands and 26 m high on the north and south.

The distinctive elliptical, saddle-shaped roof involves two separate structural systems. The primary three-dimensional 'cable-net structure' – comprising twelve 70 m high, cigar-shaped, tubular steel masts on the perimeter, high-strength backstay rods, and spiral strand forestay and tension-ring cables – provides primary support to the roof by resisting gravity, wind uplift and lateral loads. The secondary or roof-plate system comprises box section rafters, radially arranged at approximately 8 m centres, and supporting rod steel purlins that in turn support standing seam and polycarbonate roof cladding.

Natural light enters the stands along the perimeter of the concrete bowl, and transparent polycarbonate along the inner edge of the roof allows light through to the pitch. Adjustable louver vents in the high-level corner voids above the stand allow the airflow through the stadium to be varied.

On each side of the stadium is a service and circulation tower accommodating the ramps that serve as the main routes to the stands. The towers also house many of the building's services – WCs, main plant, electrical services and boiler plant.

Spacious internal concourses provide for circulation inside the stadium, and an external civic space around the building comprises hard and soft landscaping and seating at the base of the columns. A mix of uses – a sports institute, shops, leisure areas and bars – surrounds this plaza.

↑   Views to the pitch and opposing stands on a crowded match day

↗   Sections showing the stadium's phased design, initially for the Commonwealth Games athletics event (left), followed by the stadium's subsequent use for football (right)

↗↗   Elegant access ramps, providing for safe, comfortable entry and egress

What the City of Manchester Stadium shows

Comfort, convenience and safety

In its effective conception for crowd management, the design of the stadium's circulation systems is pivotal. The entry ramps allow crowds to enter and leave the stadium quickly and safely, and their gentle gradient – 1 in 20 (1 in 12 inside) – facilitates access by wheelchair users. Innovation in turnstile design, configured with a 120° rotor arm, offers users increased space when entering the stadium. These factors combine to provide a reassuring arrival experience. They also reduce queuing times and pre-match agitation – in turn decreasing operational costs as ticketing controllers are not required.

An innovative fire strategy, using double roller shutters without a sprinkler system and containing many services in the towers, enabled the creation of continuous concourses. These allow for mass evacuation and provide large, clean, uncluttered spaces for users' ease of movement to the concessions and WCs that are spread around the building, avoiding the typical half-time scramble for refreshment and relief. These spacious concourses, designed as 'streets', meet the project objectives for coherence, clarity and user amenity.

Fine viewing conditions

A fundamental objective is for the spectator to see the event! The column-free cable-net roof structure enables everyone to view the track, pitch or arena without obstructions. This is aided by a recessed tread on the gangways that reduces adjacent handrail heights and ensures unimpeded viewing. In addition to the important good views of events, the views of the building from the stand – with the sweeping arcs of the lower tiers and the roof – are exhilarating.

The required seating bias determined a bowl with high sides on the east and west and low ends on the north and south, allowing a single roof geometry to cover all the seating. The structure leaves large areas in the corners which can be opened for pitch ventilation when the stadium is not in use. The stadium's high sides offer players and spectators protection from prevailing winds and low sun angles, whilst enabling the majority of seats to be in the areas most favoured by spectators. The low sides also allow maximum sun onto the grassed pitch. The fine experience set by these conditions is enhanced by the natural light that suffuses the stands, entering through the upper edge of the concrete bowl, the roof opening and the roof's transparent inside edge.

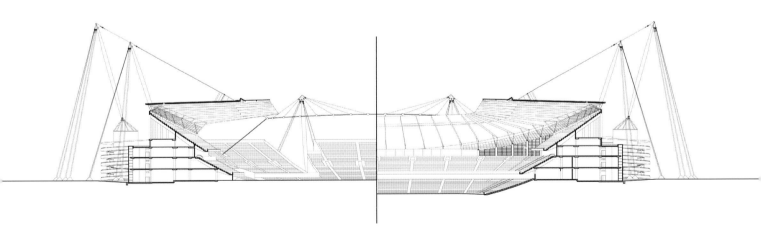

The fine experience set by these conditions is enhanced by the natural light that suffuses the stands, entering through the upper edge of the concrete bowl, the roof opening and the roof's transparent inside edge.

Phased change in requirements

A successful two-stage design approach enabled the stadium to meet its initial requirements as an athletics venue, before adaptation for its permanent use for football. To provide the running track for the Commonwealth Games, the stadium had to be elongated. The first stage of construction involved completion of three sides of the permanent stadium, with a temporary stand to make up the rest of the seating for the duration of the Games. In the second phase, the track was removed, the ground lowered by 6 m, with 90,000 cu m of earth removed, a lower section installed to provide 24 additional rows of seating and the temporary stand replaced. The bowl, which first covered three-quarters of the stadium in a horseshoe shape, was completed for the football stadium. The primary mast and cable structural system – totally independent of the roof plate structure – was fully constructed in the initial phase. The secondary structure was finalised with the construction of the north stand in the second phase. The project shows the value that can be attained by strategic design for one-off events, avoiding the redundancy associated with 'white elephants'.

Sustained effectiveness

The stadium provides excellent conditions for spectators, with fine spatial quality. Its scale and striking form are powerful in place-making. The achievements meet the project's regeneration objectives in a sustainable way.

Place-making

The stadium's striking sculptural form provides a strong image and fine sightlines from within and without. As one approaches the building, the views towards it terminate the key view corridors, helping to define its sense of place. The building also responds to local context – the canal corridor and the housing south of Ashton New Road.

The elliptical form is oriented so as to place the stadium's tallest parts in the middle of the site, whilst the lower northern and southern aspects acknowledge the sensitive neighbouring uses. The objective for the stadium to be part of a lively local setting is partly assured by its incorporation in the new Sportcity complex, with the leisure and residential functions that are included in the overall development.

↖ The stadium as a 'place-maker' (above and below), signified by its sculptural masts, ramps and elliptical roof

↗ Plans for the stadium's two successive uses: athletics (left) and football (right)

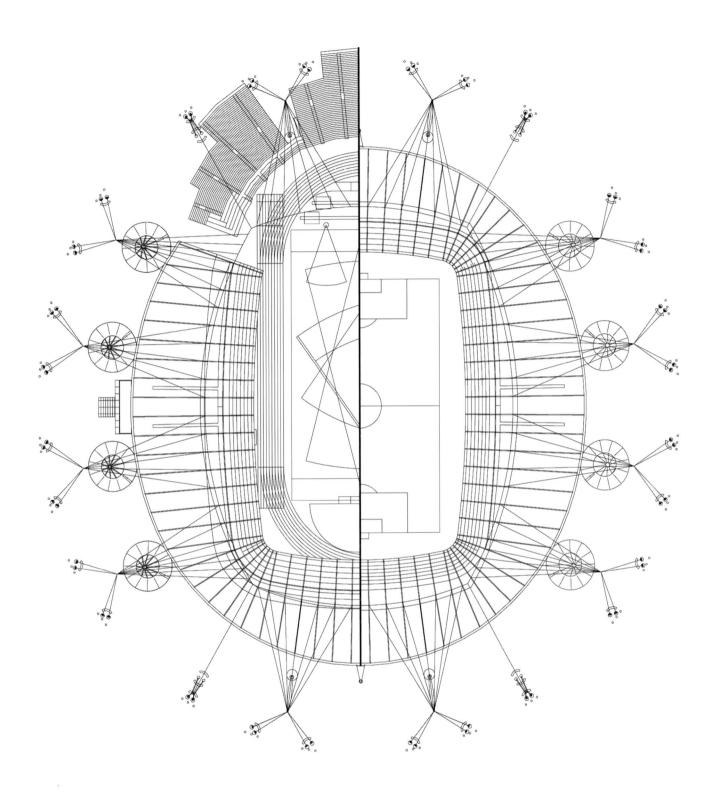

ARCHITECTS
Arup Associates

CLIENT
Manchester City Council

PROJECT ADDRESS
Sportcity
Manchester M11 3FF

AWARDS
2003
Institution of Civil Engineers
   (North West Merit Award)
Institution of Structural Engineers
   Structural Awards (Structural
   Special Award)
Building Services Award
Structural Steel Design Award

2002
British Construction Industry
   Major Project Award
   (High Commendation)
Manchester Civic Society
   Renaissance Award
   (Joint Winner)
City Life Awards (Building of the Year)

EMI GROUP HEADQUARTERS

Skilfully adapted 1980s building, incorporating an effectively proportioned, well-lit atrium that works as a lively heart

The EMI headquarters offers highly stimulating and supportive workplace accommodation in a previously redundant office building. With important changes to the entrance and façade, and the far-reaching transformation of a central open courtyard into a wonderful covered atrium, the building demonstrates the scope to invigorate outdated properties and render them relevant to contemporary needs. The project shows imaginative use of lighting, and the creation of varied internal settings that avert a 'corporate' interior feel, within a consistent visual framework.

The brief

EMI needed a global headquarters to accommodate some 320 staff from four different parts of its business that were occupying different buildings. The new building's role was to facilitate efficiency by locating operations together, enhance communication between departments, and serve as a flagship, with a distinct, contemporary work environment that engendered a sense of community and promoted awareness of EMI's brand to its staff and the public.

The structure selected for the new headquarters offered 10,000 sq m of space arranged around a lifeless courtyard. The designers worked closely with representatives across EMI to identify requirements and in following through the design development to details of interior specification. The aesthetic sought was clean and functional, with the design conveying an appropriately balanced image between a music company and global corporation. The project was also aimed at being effective environmentally. A significant aspect of this objective was the decision to recycle the building, for which the brief involved opening it up internally and creating the new workspace and social areas.

← Animated atrium with lively activity at its base, varied treatments on the internal elevations, views through to the work space beyond, and the play of light and shadow

→ Further sources of interest and vitality: the exposed lifts, the passing clouds overhead, and their reflection in the atrium glazing

Overview

The six-storey building, on a side street in Kensington, is entered through a new full-height curved glass façade enclosing the corner that addresses Kensington High Street. Behind this, the building was stripped back to the structure. The double-height reception area, formed by removing part of the first floor slab, is a dramatic space. A backlit glass reception desk forms a strong focal point and large screens playing music video footage project EMI through the glazed elevation. The spacious foyer leads to meeting rooms, a highly specified 'listening room' – an independent box-in-box structure for acoustic performance – and an elegant curved timber staircase up to the base of the atrium at first-floor level. The rear part of the ground floor is a loading and service area.

The atrium is key to the building's success. This well-lit, uplifting, flexible space is used for a wide variety of functions, including live performances, seminars, conferences, corporate and informal parties, as well as dining and meetings. Its proportions are generous and easy to animate – 10.5 m by 21 m and five storeys high. Its new glass roof, angled for water run-off, maximises daylight, and its elevations have been substantially opened up, with two clad in white-glazed brick and two with full-height glazing. Balconies project into the volume, bringing movement into the space at all levels, and contributing to the sense of connection between the atrium and the workspace zones behind its elevations.

The play of light and shadow from the roof structure beyond the glazed light panels contributes further visual interest.

What the EMI Headquarters shows

A living atrium

Spatially, visually and in terms of activity, the building centres on the bright, naturally lit, glass-covered atrium. The treatment of the atrium elevations responds to all the brief objectives, with the white-glazed brick surfaces enhancing brightness, whilst providing a textured surface that not only avoids a sense of clinical sterility but also offers subtle visual interest. It contributes further by allowing for the play of shadow from the roof structure beyond the glazed roof panels.

The cuts through the atrium elevations create a series of large openings, varying in size. These provide a visual rhythm in the aspect across the atrium and the views to the workplace settings beyond them. The approach depended on a new fire safety strategy that enabled the atrium to be opened up to floor plates at all levels.

As the setting for the restaurant and the building's main social hub, the base of the atrium is assured as a lively place, whether one is in it or looking down from above. The introduction of wireless technology through the building, giving people extensive flexibility in where they work, increases the ways in which they use the atrium. The space is further animated by the balconies that overlook it from above, and by the new exposed lift shaft inserted in one corner. The balconies offer further variation within the controlled vocabulary applied to the space.

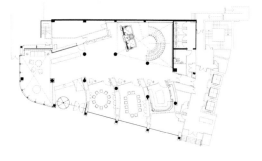

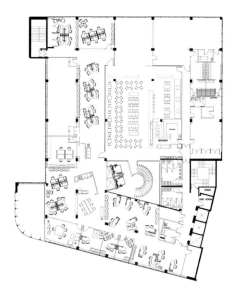

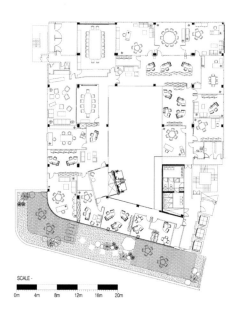

SCALE

0m   4m   8m   12m   16m   20m

↖ The sculptural staircase up from the ground floor reception area to the atrium base at first floor level

← Double-height reception area projecting the ambience inside the building through the new curved glass façade

↗ Floor plans: entrance level (top), atrium base (middle), typical upper floor (bottom)

On the east elevation the balconies project into the volume. Between the south and west wings, timber walkways with clear glazed fronts have been bolted on to enable circulation that bypasses the WCs and original building core.

The galleries, walkways and large openings in the elevations enable people to see activity across the atrium volume as well as from floor to floor, contributing to the sense of community sought by the brief. Together these features ensure that the views up the atrium are always dynamic – lifts moving vertically, people moving horizontally and clouds passing overhead. Open grille bridges between the new lifts and the floor plate enhance the sense of connection, by providing views to the floor below. With an aerobics studio sited adjacent to the dining area on the atrium base, behind a 7 m sliding wall, the lively central space can be further expanded.

The sliding wall's unusual cellbond composition, constructed from a honeycomb of aluminium filled with resin and clad on both sides in 4 mm acrylic, provides several benefits. When closed, natural light still passes through, but the cells act as multiple tiny kaleidoscopes, obscuring the view behind them, and contributing textural and visual interest in themselves. This lightweight material enables the door to be moved easily by one person.

Use of light
The distinctive influence of lighting is linked to a clear lighting brief, which sought to maximise natural light, provide a cool, diffused solution and ensure a comfortable working environment. Natural light enters through the atrium roof and the perimeter windows. The arrangement of the generously proportioned top-lit central atrium, surrounded by floors of 12 m depth, promotes reliance on natural light and enables the building to feel very open.

The proportion of enclosed space – some 40 per cent – could have countered this effect, a result that is avoided by the use of glazed partitions to enclose the front of the offices.

The atrium presented the main lighting challenge. Its provision of ambient natural light for the workspace zones furthest from the building perimeter is subject to changes over the course of a day. Its wide range of uses – café, cosy 'snug' area, evening functions, and for some larger events its extension into the adjacent studio – have varying requirements. The lighting strategy harnesses varied light sources in all the building's settings, with differences in the mix between them generating variety in the mood and identity of the various spaces, and scope to change a setting's ambience according to use and time of day. This underpins the rich repertoire of lighting solutions that are used in addition to natural light. These range from the UV-bonded glass counters with LEDs – making them colour-changing light boxes that serve as strong visual foci in the reception area and café – through halogen and fluorescent ceiling luminaires, floor lights, uplighters on walls, pendant lights, desk lights and backlit glass, to the distinctive slender light boxes that incorporate fluorescent tubes, providing an elegant, exciting line of blue light around each floor.

The atrium really is this building's beating heart, benefiting from converging strategies that ensure it is attractive, well used and animated.

← View of atrium showing white glazed brick elevations

↗ Work areas (left and right), offering local variety in look and feel, within the building's consistent spatial framework

Corporate and team identity

The design strategy enables the occupying departments to ring changes in identity. This draws on colours, finishes and accent lighting to convey differences in character, and to lend variety in local feel. As the overall building is unified by a consistent overall spatial framework based on similarities in layout and the positioning of elements such as breakout areas and refreshment points, the interior remains coherent and highly legible, despite the approach to varied visual expression in the respective user areas. The simultaneous feeling of being anchored in a clearly organised matrix whilst able to enjoy a degree of looseness and variety at the level of individual work groups and teams is of value to building users.

The achievement in maintaining a strong sense of legibility alongside freedom of expression is reinforced by being able to walk right round the floor plate and see through the permeable atrium elevations. This successful outcome meets the mutually conflicting requirements of the brief – the staff aspiration for the building to have a 'non-corporate feel', and the executives' requirement for it to be 'professional and business like'. With its range of more formal areas and more relaxed spaces, notably the almost domestic social spaces in the team areas, the design achieves an effective balance.

Sustainable regeneration

The EMI building is a major success in recycling a building, rewarding the vision shown when its potential was identified and its scope envisaged. The investment in the structure has not only extended the building's life, but also created an exciting space with a memorable sense of place. The atrium really is this building's beating heart, benefiting from converging strategies that ensure it is attractive, well used and animated. The project demonstrates a successful approach to designing effective settings that people can appropriate and overlay with their own references. From the reception through the atrium and workspace to the external roof deck, all the settings express vitality. The EMI building exemplifies sustainable regeneration, underpinned by facilitative design and spatial organisation.

DESIGNERS
MoreySmith

CLIENT
EMI Group

PROJECT ADDRESS
EMI Headquarters
27 Wrights Lane
London W8 5SW

AWARDS
British Council for Offices, 2004
– Regional and National Winner,
Refurbished / Recycled Workplace
category
DBA Design Effectiveness Award,
2004 – Office and Commercial
Interiors category

ERCOL

A strategically arranged sequence of design, manufacturing and sales settings, enabling all workers to feel part of the factory's overall design enterprise, whilst enjoying extensive natural light and direct views to the external landscape

The project demonstrates how intelligent rethinking of production processes – with a view to efficiency and sustainability – can facilitate use of design to meet social and environmental aims. The building's spatial organisation integrates the factory's industrial, studio, showroom and office areas, displaying the progression of activities that contribute to the overall production cycle, and revealing this narrative to all its participants. The interior offers a high standard of workplace. The factory area is suffused with natural light and enriched by its aspect to the wooded landscape outside. The critical thought applied to the manufacturing processes has also benefited the building's external setting, as the architects have achieved a measurable reduction in noise pollution relative to the factory's acoustic impact in its previous location.

The brief

Ercol is a privately owned furniture manufacturer employing some 350 people in manufacturing, design, administration and sales. After operating from a number of sites in the High Wycombe area, the company sought to accommodate all its activities in one building. A new building also offered scope to project and evolve Ercol's brand. Ercol's staff are valued for their specialist craft-based skills and their long-standing involvement with the company; a parallel project objective was to provide good, open working conditions for them all.

A site of some 9.5 ha was acquired in a wooded setting next to Princes Risborough Railway Station, with the largest plot – four ha adjacent to a public footpath that crosses the site – selected for the factory. The vision was for a building that would retain the landscape, including a number of protected trees, as the dominant element.

These aspirations, and others, were encapsulated in clear briefing objectives. They focused on functional integration, an open ethos, Ercol's image and brand – based on design, craftsmanship and materials – and best value from the project budget.

A set of technical objectives centred on streamlining Ercol's production flow, optimising relationships between the constituent functions, minimising waste, reducing the need for cooling, delivering other aspects of energy efficiency and reducing noise. The latter was also a planning concern. A strong focus was placed on design and cost engineering to achieve value without compromising design quality.

The factory in its setting: panoramic view of the building's wooded surroundings from the production floor

Overview

The Ercol building is a 'low slung' pavilion of 15,000 sq m gross area, configured as a large rectangle. The building is approached through, and framed by, an old avenue of beech, maple, horse chestnut and other trees. Heralding one's arrival is an outer, open, beamed structure that projects from the glazed front elevation. The building is arranged as a series of layers that accommodate Ercol's internal functions. From the entrance, and advancing into the interior, the sequence reads as reception, showroom and gallery space, followed by the large factory.

The building's two-storey 2,580 sq m front section accommodates the showroom, office area – mostly open plan – design studio and restaurant. A double-volume, top-lit, slender atrium, and a restaurant for use by customers, staff and visitors, mediate the transition between the single-height spaces and the larger 11,490 sq m double-height factory area.

The structure is a 180 m by 90 m steel frame, on a 22.5 m by 12 m grid, to an eaves height of 7.2 m, supported on simple pad foundations. The very low angle, 1°, portal frame creates the appearance of a pavilion, rather than a shed. The structure for the first floor offices is a separate steel frame, on a 7.5 m module, supporting a concrete slab on metal decking.

The office and showroom area is mainly enclosed by curtain walling, with areas of externally rendered and insulated solid blockwork wall. The enclosure to the factory is external colour-coated (pvf2) steel cladding, horizontally aligned, and supported on galvanised steel posts that rise from the floor slab to the roof. The walls are insulated with 130 mm rockwool and perforated internal cladding for acoustic and thermal buffering.

The roof is a single-ply membrane over 130 mm rockwool insulation on a perforated-steel deck, providing thermal insulation as well as sound insulation and absorption on a similar basis to the walls.

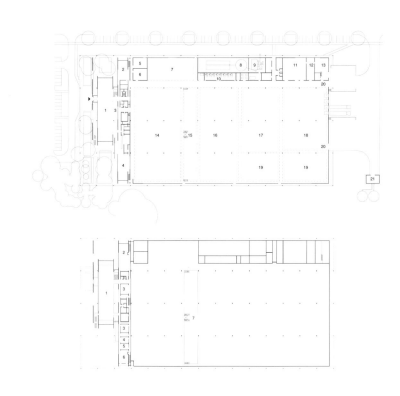

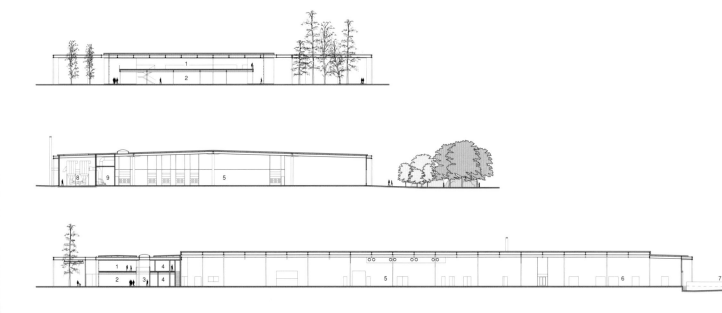

What the Ercol building shows

Spatial narrative

The Ercol project demonstrates the beneficial outcome that can follow from clear vision, rigour in meeting objectives and coherent physical design. The building's spatial organisation reveals the sequence of activities involved in the overall process it supports, offering participants and visitors an appreciation of all aspects of the enterprise's success, and fostering recognition of everyone's role.

The design provides for strong functional association and visual integration. The design studio in the office zone is close to the jigshop in the factory area below, enabling rapid access between the two. The chairman's office, next to the boardroom and close to the open-plan office area, has a view to the factory. A direct staircase linking the offices and factory facilitates easy transfer and testing between those workers involved in generating ideas and those responsible for production.

The factory staff can see into the showroom and restaurant from the production environment, and the showroom and upper viewing gallery provide a view of the entire manufacturing operation, commencing with the delivery of timber, and proceeding through machining, assembly, polishing, drying and upholstery, to packing and shipment.

This narrative, revealed as one moves through the manufacturing space, is almost entirely legible from the viewing gallery on the upper level of the building's two-storey section. The gallery offers internal views to the showroom and a dramatic view of the double-height factory (despite obstruction of a complete view by a temporary 690 sq m storage mezzanine constructed across the short section between the machining and assembly areas), as well as vistas of the external landscape to the north and south, and external views to the outer structure that forms a courtyard with mature trees and a woodland shelter belt beyond.

The building's spatial organisation reveals the sequence of activities involved in the overall process it supports, offering participants and visitors an appreciation of all aspects of the enterprise's success, and fostering recognition of everyone's role.

↖ Plans: ground floor (top) and upper floor (below)

← Cross-sections: through the offices (top), through the factory (middle); long section (bottom)

↑ Two views of the factory: from outside in (top), from inside out (below)

Spatial quality in the factory

Ercol's workers have the benefit of fine spatial quality both in the 'office' space and the factory. Natural light and enriching landscaped views are important benefits in the building's internal spaces. Whilst these attributes are increasingly sought in the design of office environments, the high standard of workplace accommodation achieved at Ercol is notable, as most of the building comprises factory space. The polycarbonate rooflight that runs down the length of the factory roof close to its northeast edge is key to this achievement. It is supplemented by a 3.7 m high, 120 m long solar-control glass window incorporated in the long southwest elevation opposite. In combination these features enable good natural light in the factory and a wonderful external view. Given that Ercol's workers are engaged in producing timber furniture, the wooded views that these windows frame have particular relevance.

Environmental achievements

Alongside its provision for natural light, the building is designed for solar control, with a range of passive devices, including screens, louvers, canopies, a balcony and projecting fin walls. These enable summertime operations to take place in both the factory and office settings without the use of air-conditioning.

Other civic and environmental benefits relate to design features that reduce noise and dust. Dust and waste wood for recycling are stored in a 200 cu m silo. Efficient burning of wood waste provides all hot water and heating, requiring little or no use of fossil fuels for these purposes.

The fine spatial quality, natural light and landscaped views enjoyed in the building interior set a distinctive standard for factory environments.

The elimination of internal compartmentation in the production area enables the benefits of open-plan operation to be achieved across the factory's production area. This was made possible by working with Ercol's suppliers to substitute lacquers based on volatile organic compounds (VOCs) with non-flammable water-based alternatives to spray the furniture.

For a business that is typically very noisy, the sound insulation has been measurably successful. The design treatment – including solid blockwork internal enclosures to house noisy fans – has helped to limit noise pollution to the residences that lie on three sides of the building. This compares favourably to Ercol's acoustic impact in its previous accommodation, and to readings in other factories that use similar equipment.

Implicit branding

The building itself expresses the image that Ercol seeks – refined but unpretentious. The materials and colour palette play a part in this – externally, white structure, light-grey cladding and extensive glazing, and internally, light timber and white plaster in the atrium, restaurant, offices and showroom, with white perforated-steel cladding and grey power-floated concrete floor in the factory. The building's integral relationship with the existing external landscape and new planting directly outside gives it a special sense of place and a close affinity to its work. The most powerful signal of Ercol's commitment to its products is the building's spatial arrangement that celebrates all the contributors to its processes of furniture design and production.

↖ Slender atrium mediating the single-height office, showroom and studio spaces and the double-height factory space

↗ Embracing the wooded setting: beams projecting from the glazed entrance

ARCHITECTS
Horden Cherry Lee Architects

CLIENT
Ercol Holdings Ltd

PROJECT ADDRESS
Ercol Furniture Factory
Summerleys Road
Princes Risborough
Buckinghamshire HP27 9PX

AWARDS
Civic Trust Award, 2003
Malcolm Dean Award
   (Wycombe District council), 2003
RIBA Award, 2003
SEDA Sustainable Business
   Award, 2003
Times / Gestetner Digital and Office
   Collection, 2003

ISSEY MIYAKE STORE, MAYFAIR

Refined retail space offering a delicate interplay of light and shadow, calm and motion, exterior and interior views

In an age of increasing visual saturation, especially in city centres, and with approaches to retail design that seek to 'rev up' stimulation, this store just off Regent Street provides a distinctive contrast. The design crosses retail and gallery concepts – positioning the garments as artistic objects, to be glimpsed, then viewed and touched. By creating a strong visual connection between the store's interior and its external urban setting, the designers have dissolved the barrier between outside and in, in a way that invites entry and facilitates exploration. The serene interior offers a well-balanced combination of stimulus and repose, with a controlled palette of finishes and good execution. The overall result is a masterclass in permeability and enclosure, animation and reflection, and skilful modulation of light and shadow.

The brief

The Issey Miyake store was designed to occupy the ground floor and basement of a five-storey existing building on the corner of Conduit Street and Savile Row. With the building's small footprint of some 20 m by 10 m, the design needed to open up the space. More permeability was needed both between the ground and lower-ground floors, and between the interior and exterior of the store. Given the distinctive nature of Issey Miyake's fine garments and the character of this part of Mayfair as a locale for art galleries, the vision set for the store was as a bridge between art and fashion. Nevertheless, it is a store, for which the design aim was to create a 'luminous and fluid space that invites participation', with a view to customers conceiving the merchandise as objects of desire.

← View of the store from the entrance area, with staircase to the lower ground floor (left)

→ Strong sense of connection from the lower ground to the ground floor above

Overview

The store's two principal elevations of 7 m and 17 m – on Conduit Street and Savile Row – now have large visual openings at street level. This has been achieved by inserting a series of large glazed panels, 6.5 m wide and 3.5 m high, on Conduit Street, and panels of equal height – some 4 m, some 6 m wide – on Savile Row. The 1.5 m wide corner entrance is angled to these streets at 45°, with a 3.8 m high glazed door occupying the full width.

The third, mostly solid, elevation forms the rear wall to the ground-floor changing rooms. The fourth wall adjoins the adjacent property, with the entirely internal elevation along this line forming the store's main interior backdrop. The project entailed removing part of the ground-floor slab, to open up the basement to daylight and connect this space to the ground floor.

The rationalisation of space at ground level and the integration of the basement with the main space have resulted in a spatial quality of clarity and great fluidity.

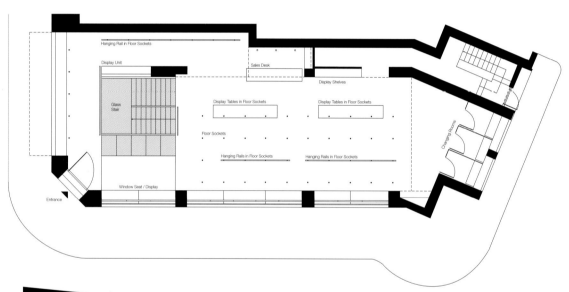

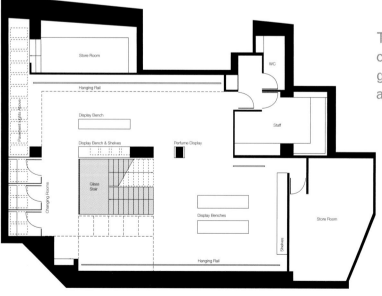

The interior gives one a sense of being centred and 'in touch'. It also sets off the garments with a clarity that fosters their appreciation.

↖   Floor plans: ground floor (above); lower ground (below)

→   Dissolving the barrier between inside and out: continuously changing external vista from within the store

What the Issey Miyake store shows

Inviting participation

The successful achievement in inviting participation hinges on the visual relation that has been created between the store interior and its external setting. In the main, this derives from the openings that have been inserted into the principal elevations, with the views that these afford through the large glazed panels. The effect is enhanced by a series of travertine sills that serve as seats on the interior of these elevations. Made from the same material as the external cladding, these give a sense that the external façades have been folded into the interior, with the outside and inside appearing as continuous space.

This promotes the sense of spaciousness and unifies the visual connection between outside and in. With the store's internal beauty revealed to passers-by, it is poised to attract interest from the busy pedestrian and traffic movement past its corner site. Inside the store one relates to this external movement, grounding one in the recognition that the store is part of contemporary urban life despite its rarefied aura.

With part of the slab over the lower-ground floor removed, another visual dimension is apparent. The approach to the lower level – via a glass and stainless steel staircase and glass bridge – is partly visible from the street. The cutaway and the glass staircase enhance the quality of the basement space – admitting natural light and making it integral to the store. The staircase design expands the range of visual interest internally.

Simplicity, contrast and calm animation

The design of the Issey Miyake store offers extreme refinement, in an environment that is at once contemplative and welcoming. The interior gives one a sense of being centred and 'in touch'. It also sets off the garments with a clarity that fosters their appreciation.

The ground floor is a 4.5 m high space, almost entirely without columns. It has a marked sense of calm, deriving from the controlled palette of finishes and colour – white marmarino (plaster and marble mix) walls, a white ceiling and light-grey concrete floor.

The interior is suffused with natural light from the principal and entrance elevations, on which the ratio of glazing to opacity is some 95 per cent. The third street-facing elevation admits light through etched glazing, giving privacy to the changing rooms sited along this wall. The changing rooms on the lower-ground floor also have the benefit of natural light, with their location below glass blocks in the pavement above.

The fourth elevation is solid, and forms the major plane on which light is reflected. This long surface is modulated, with recesses that keep the vertical structural elements visually contained, and contribute to the composition of light and shadow. Here the marmarino finish has been applied to create smooth and textured surfaces, accentuating variety in their reflection of light and the play of shadows.

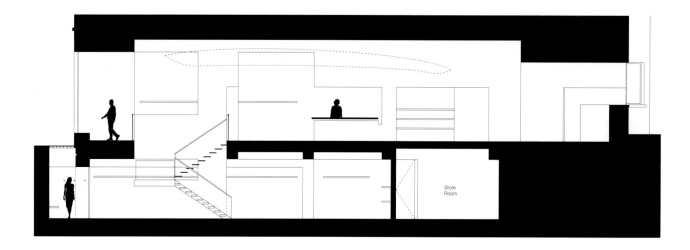

This provides rich interest, and the diurnal and seasonal changes in daylight levels and sun position generate continuous variations in luminosity. Light is also reflected from the floor, with the vein in the tiles affording further interest.

The clarity and simplicity of the white plaster wall forms the store's predominant backdrop to the garments, which are displayed individually and in several series on racks. The setting highlights their rich colours and their sculptural folds, lending them a jewel-like quality that enhances their appeal.

Further animation is provided by people in the space, with the spare but glowing surfaces setting them off as mobile sculptural forms. The opening to the floor below, directly inside the entrance, enhances this effect; on each floor one has sight of people arriving from the other and walking across the landing between the flights of stairs.

The bridge and stairs help to animate the space below, as movement is visible overhead through their translucent glass. Similarly, the movement of people walking on the pavement can be seen through the glass blocks above the lower-ground-floor changing rooms.

↑   Long section, showing inter-relationship of the two floors, and the use of space below the pavement as a changing area

←   View from the entrance area, with the travertine sills below the large glazed panels in the elevation mediating the boundary between outside and in

↗   View from the rear of the ground floor, with the play of light and shadow enriched by the sculptural lighting feature

Sculptural lighting
A distinctive steel mesh ceiling feature, commissioned from the lighting designer Ingo Maurer, combines great delicacy with a strong presence and adds to the experience of movement in the store. Twelve gold-coloured ventilators in its cylindrical body generate air movement that causes hundreds of silver leaves that hang beneath the cylinder to flutter. The shadows of the leaves falling on the plastered wall surfaces also move, providing still more stimulus and interest.

The Issey Miyake store reveals itself in a confident but quiet manner. In a hectic urban setting where vendors compete for attention with visual thrust, design that invites rather than bombards is important. This stance is also shown in the store's displays. These never fill the window spaces. Instead they allow generous views into, out of and through the glazing, referencing the urban life of which the store – and its fashion merchandise – form a gracious part.

ARCHITECTS
Stanton Williams

CLIENT
Issey Miyake London Ltd

PROJECT ADDRESS
52 Conduit Street
Mayfair
London W1S 2YX

JERWOOD VANBRUGH THEATRE, RADA

A highly creative new building for the Royal Academy of Dramatic Art, inserted on a narrow, deep site in Bloomsbury, showing imagination and rigour in providing excellent performance spaces and associated facilities for production, teaching and public audiences

The new building housing the Jerwood Vanbrugh Theatre fronts onto Malet Street. Its skilful arrangement accommodates a significant range of high-quality performance and support areas in confined space. The main theatre is masterful in its sense of spaciousness and its scope for reconfiguration. A highly stimulating and beautifully crafted glass-covered vertical shaft brings daylight into the building's deeper zones and demonstrates a commitment to rich user experience. The project also involved the substantial remodelling of the academy's existing building that faces Gower Street, and the provision of links between this and the new building, integrating RADA's accommodation on the combined site.

The brief

The Jerwood Vanbrugh Theatre building provides two theatres, a foyer with box office, bar and café, rehearsal rooms, studios, workshops, offices and other support facilities. It occupies two-thirds of a site that extends 55 m east–west between Malet and Gower Streets, with five additional metres' length below ground level. The site for the new building was made available by demolishing RADA's original Malet Street theatre, first built in 1921, then partly destroyed during the Second World War and rebuilt in 1954 with a 500-seat auditorium that proved to be too large and inadequate acoustically.

The brief for the new building required a design that would qualify for a public entertainment licence in its performance and assembly areas, and provide an expanded array of new facilities, with minimal impact on the adjacent properties. This limited the new building's height, increasing the challenge in providing all the facilities required on the narrow, 15.4 m, site. Another requirement was to link the new building with the retained building facing Gower Street. Although RADA had occupied the whole block for some 70 years, the previous Malet Street building had been connected to the building facing Gower Street only at basement and flytower levels.

Strategies to improve RADA's accommodation had been under consideration for many years. Funding for the new building's construction was enabled by the award of a lottery grant in 1995, coupled with significant private donations. The overall project also involved significant upgrading of RADA's Gower Street building that backs onto the new building.

← The cleft at the transition between RADA's academy and public spaces: affording external connection from and daylight to the building's deeper zones, and visual linkages between the surrounding spaces

Overview

The new building fully occupies the narrow site and extends to within one metre of the Gower Street building. It comprises ten storeys of accommodation, three below ground level. The public Malet Street entrance is signalled by its symmetrical elevation comprising a well-lit convex bay clad in glass panels and a terracotta-tiled façade above the third-floor level. One enters the building into an open foyer and café space for circulation and 'milling'. To allow for this open space at ground level on the constrained site, the new 203-seat Vanbrugh Theatre is situated at second-floor level, with the smaller new John Gielgud Theatre in the basement, along with production spaces such as the scene workshops. The flytower is located immediately behind the Malet Street elevation, with the space between this and the Gower Street building covered by a vaulted metal roof.

What the Jerwood Vanbrugh Theatre shows

Historic reference, current functionality

The strategic approach to RADA's Bloomsbury infrastructure put considerable value on the historical associations of the Gower Street building. These include sculptures by Eric Gill over the entrance, plaques over the grand staircase that commemorate some of Britain's finest actors who had been trained at the academy, and a theatre named after George Bernard Shaw in recognition of his significant endowments to the institution. The wish to perpetuate this built legacy underlay the decision to retain this smaller building, adapt it to house the main administrative and teaching spaces, and invest in the larger new building to provide the requisite facilities for the academy's work in the 21st century.

Space to support technical performance

All the new facilities provided are central to the academy's needs, but the prize asset is surely the main theatre. For the audience, this space feels wonderful, with the viewer placed in an immediate and engaging relationship with the stage. For student performers, the facility serves to inspire and teach. Inserted into a remarkably compact space, the Jerwood Vanbrugh Theatre feels considerably larger than it is.

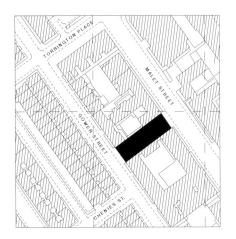

↑   Site context between Gower and Malet Streets

↗   Malet Street elevation, with the lower glazed convex façade expressing the building's public theatre function

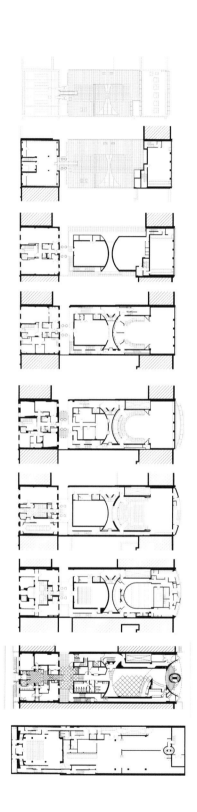

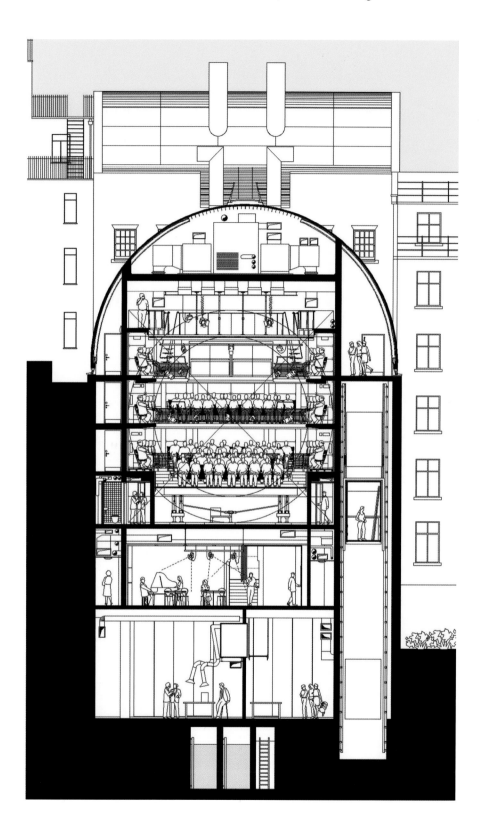

↖ Sequence of plans: from basement (bottom) to roof (top)

↑ Section through new Malet Street building showing the theatre and variety of other functions it accommodates

The theatre's effectiveness relates firstly to its proportions. These are derived from a 17th-century design by Inigo Jones, with the auditorium form intersecting that of the stage and flytower, both in plan and section. The stalls, circle and two balconies account for the theatre's four levels, lending a lofty sense of volume to the space, despite floor-to-floor heights of only 2.25 m, and the requirement to accommodate contemporary building services. The enhanced spatial perception is a design achievement, relating largely to the construction of the balcony fronts in yacht wire. The avoidance of solid mass on the balcony fronts has the effect of shifting the limiting enclosure in the space outward to the theatre walls. The twin advantage to viewers is the intimacy of a small theatre combined with a sense of spatial expansiveness. The benefit to the student performers is learning to hold the stage in a theatre that seems considerably larger than this one is or needs to be.

Flexibility to support functional objectives

The theatre's flexibility in terms of spatial configuration contributes significantly to its educational value. The format can be changed from thrust to proscenium, from apron to 'in-the-round'. This is facilitated by a hydraulically powered, seven-piece floor with numerous hinged flaps on each side of the stage, enabling the base of the space to be altered from flat format to alternative proscenia with an orchestra pit. In addition, a tension wire grid at 70 mm centres above the stage facilitates access by technicians to vary the sets and lighting.

The other facilities in the new building are also valuable assets to RADA, as are the suite of enhanced facilities in the Gower Street building, including the restructured GBS Theatre. The circulation routes between the two buildings at all levels on the northern and southern edges of the floor plate enable their respective facilities to be well linked.

↑ Theatre in use for a social gathering (top); view of the stage and wire-fronted balconies, creating the sense of expansiveness inside the theatre (middle); optimising conditions in which the student actors can develop their performance skills (bottom)

Crafted space that suggests and delights
The design strategy has delivered more
than functional excellence and the
perpetuation of tradition. The overall
site divides into thirds, with a lightwell
at each juncture. Where the old and
new buildings almost join, the lightwell
is conventional, but a striking vertical
feature, known as the 'cleft', marks
the transition between the public and
academy spaces in the new building.
This has an important functional purpose
in bringing daylight into the building's
deeper zones, and, through a glazed
floor, to the basement. It is also a gem
at the heart of the building. A cascade
of light seen from all the floors, the cleft
provides external connection and visual
linkages between the varied spaces
that surround it, fostering continual
awareness of the building's rich
offerings. This experience is integral.
Circulation routes run by the extensive
glazing that encloses the cleft, and
window seats are built into its elevations,
affording their use as study spaces or
places for reflection. With the care in
its articulation, this slender atrium is
almost a building in its own right. It plays
a powerful role in integrating the overall
suite of facilities and the respective
floors, and it does so in a poetic spirit
that suggests 'it's because you're worth
it'. In addition to its enrichment of the
building's daily use, the cleft offers a
distinctive additional experience when
the sun hits Jacob Epstein's bust of
George Bernard Shaw at its base at
12 minutes to 12 on the summer
solstice.

In an age when such a feature typically
risks being 'value-engineered' out
of construction, the cleft is powerful
in demonstrating the value of such a
gesture, in the pleasure, interest and
organisational focus that it adds to the
building and one's experience in using
the space.

This design approach is also reflected in
the axial shift on the ground-level route
between the Malet and Gower Street
entrances. It demonstrates the potential
of design to nourish users' engagement
with a building and to stimulate
exploration.

It demonstrates the potential of design to nourish
users' engagement with a building and to stimulate
exploration.

↗ The theatre's ground floor café and milling
space, with the route to the rest of RADA's
facilities to the rear

ARCHITECTS
Avery Associates Architects

CLIENT
Royal Academy of Dramatic Art
(RADA)

PROJECT ADDRESS
Jerwood Vanbrugh Theatre
Malet Street
London WC1E 6ED

AWARDS
The ADAPT Trust Access Award, 2001
Camden Design Award, 2001
RIBA Award, 2001
British Institute of Architectural
  Technologists Open Award,
  2002 – Technical Excellence in
  Architectural Technology
Civic Trust Commendation, 2002
FX Interior Design Award, 2002
Camden Building Quality Award for
  Excellence in Inclusive Design, 2003
United States Institute of Theatre
  Technicians Award, 2003

THE MAILBOX

A highly meshed integration of varied building uses within a single building complex, mediating the contrasting urban conditions that set the context for its opposing elevations, and offering direct outdoor experience of the building's canalside setting

The Mailbox harnesses a redundant industrial building to provide an inspired example of urban regeneration and mixed use. With its vertical and horizontal arrangement of residential, retail, office, broadcasting, hotel, restaurant and bar accommodation, the building demonstrates the scope to achieve an intensive approach to integrated accommodation for diverse functions, creating a lively place. It also demonstrates an effective response to its highly varied context – the elevated city ring road that it faces and the urban canal onto which it backs, successfully addressing the variation in scale and character that these entail, whilst negotiating significant changes in site level. The design challenges 'safe' UK development practice by incorporating a central promenade that is open to the sky.

The brief

Close to Birmingham New Street railway station, The Mailbox is a major mixed-use development based on the shell of a postal sorting office constructed in the 1960s. The project fulfils the developer's aspiration to capitalise on the site's strategic location and the building's potential as a catalyst for regeneration.

Having worked with the developer on the neighbouring regeneration site at Brindleyplace, the architects were asked to help define the idea for The Mailbox before the client purchased the site. The brief was developed in an eight-week feasibility study that tested iterations of specific uses and their optimal ratio and arrangement to one another against a financial appraisal. Following the architects' appointment based on the initial project definition, they acted as concept designers developing the scheme to the point of detail design, then steering the remaining design, overseeing the construction drawings and monitoring construction quality.

The masterplan, developed as part of the feasibility study, extended beyond the site to include the route from New Street Station to the canal and the land at Salvage and Washington Wharves. The design process entailed extensive consultation with Birmingham City Planning Department, local interest groups and residents.

The accommodation was designed for tenant occupancy on a 'shell and core' basis, with the units given infrastructure for utilities and controlled points of access to ventilation systems. To facilitate vibrant fit-out design, with consistent external treatment appropriate to the base building, the architects formulated a tenant design guide. This covered maintenance of the design grid and aspects such as signage.

↖ Standing up to the elevated city ring road that runs past the building: front elevation, with the scale, massing, geometrical detailing and strong colour to establish a significant presence

Overview

The Mailbox encompasses 100,000 sq m of residential, hotel, office, leisure and retail space, including almost 40 stores and 16 bars and restaurants. Most of the eating venues are on terraces that face southwest, overlooking the waterside.

A natural granite-paved pedestrian street is cut through the heart of the building and open to the sky. This originates inside the entrance arch and forms the building's central spine. The entrance is defined by a 12 m high arch that rises to two-fifths of the height of the front elevation. On arrival from the railway station, or seen from the elevated ring road that runs past The Mailbox, the arch is the gateway to the development.

The building is arranged in three sections. From the top of the entrance staircase, the central street runs the 130 m length of the front section, flanked on both sides by 2.8 m wide arcaded promenades. These line the 520 m of frontage to 9,800 sq m of retail space accommodated on two levels.

From the entrance arch to the canal at the rear, the site rises more than 12 m. This necessitates the building's stepped plan, with the cut through it rising to 18 m above Mailbox Square, and a clear height of 6 m on the route through the building's second section that exits on the canalside.

This part of the building, with 148 m of frontage and reached via a central flight of stairs, accommodates the entrances to the offices, apartments and a group of restaurants. The remaining restaurants front directly onto three terraces that face the canal.

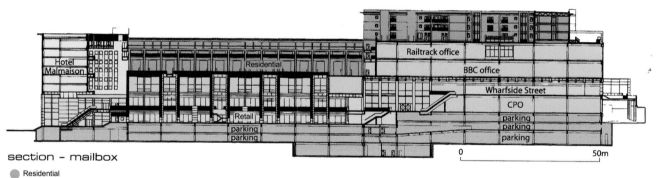

section – mailbox

- ● Residential
- ○ Hotel
- ○ Retail, Bars and Restaurants
- ● Car Parking
- ○ Office Space

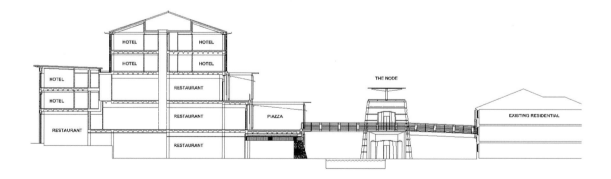

What The Mailbox shows

Contextual responsiveness

The architectural treatment is variously
bold and gentle, acknowledging the
building's contrasting settings and
defining its strong sense of place.

The front elevation is key in signifying
the new destination. A reconstituted
buff stone and glazed base with a strong
vertical motif rises to the height of the
entrance opening. Pillar-box-red render
to the five storeys above the entrance
gives The Mailbox its iconic appearance.
The coloured render is elegantly rationed,
alternating with vertical and horizontal
glazed panels above the portal. Another
fully glazed storey, topped by a band of
metal louvers, sits under the projecting
roofline. The recessive elements
make a significant contribution to this
composition – with the transparent
and reflective properties of the glazing,
entrance stairs and perspective through
the arch integral to the initial view.

Modulating the scale

As one enters the central street, the
escalators to the upper level, the
landings and bridges above, and the
columns flanking the promenade provide
a dynamic interplay of horizontal and
vertical elements. This modulates the
building's significant mass and scale. The
colonnades of terracotta-tiled columns
extend the identity established by the
red render on the front elevation into the
heart of the building. The association
is reinforced by the terracotta cladding
to the front elevation of the building's
second main section that forms the rear
enclosure of Mailbox Square.

The columns are situated between the
individual store bays and on the outer face
of the arcade. The inner columns are set
at intervals of 6 m and rise to 17.8 m – the
height of a store plus the fascia above
its window – with the outer columns
12 m apart and rising 32 m to the roofline.

Whilst the columns reinforce the visual
cohesion and order of the plan, selective
infill of the arcade places some shop
fronts directly into view, creating a softer,
rhythmic effect along the route without
detracting from the building's legibility.

On both sides of the street, a floor of
office accommodation sits above the
upper level of shops, with residential
space above the offices. The higher levels
of the building are recessed behind the
retail façades that line the open street.
The implied cornice line diverts one's
view from the higher levels, providing a
perceived scale that resembles typical
Birmingham streets, and reinforcing the
experience of The Mailbox as continuous
public realm.

↑ Contextual responsiveness: the terraced
arrangement, promoting enjoyment of the
canalside to the building's rear

↖ Long section showing the mix of uses
accommodated within The Mailbox

↖ Section through Salvage Wharf

Variation in ambience

The masterplan optimises the disposition of The Mailbox's mix of uses relative to the surrounding area. The bold mass of the front elevation stands up confidently to the elevated road that it faces, and the vertical rhythm of columns in the shopping area behind the elevation echoes this stance. The long pedestrian route along the central street shifts the dominant axis from vertical to horizontal, with the retail frontages providing an enclosing edge.

The grouping of restaurants on the canalside further emphasises the low-slung horizontal axis of the stepped terraces. The terraces play an important role in the transition of The Mailbox from harder-edged city-oriented retail and commercial space to the more relaxed and intimate setting for waterside leisure and dining.

Although the area encompassed by The Mailbox is privately owned, it provides an open route between major nodes of the city 24 hours a day. The ambience feels public. Public access is promoted by The Mailbox development's improvements to pedestrian routes in the surrounding townscape. The 300 m route from Birmingham New Street Station to The Mailbox is enhanced by decorative tiling on the pavement, whilst the underside of the elevated road where pedestrians pass has been brightly and decoratively lit. The canalside walk from The Mailbox to a nearby convention centre also connects users to Birmingham's major urban regeneration development at Brindleyplace, via a new bridge across the canal, and an attractive ramp between The Mailbox and the towpath.

The terraces play an important role in the transition of The Mailbox from harder-edged city-oriented retail and commercial space to the more relaxed and intimate setting for waterside leisure and dining.

Scale and grids

The original sorting office provided the 12 m by 12 m column grid and 6.2 m floor-to-ceiling heights that set the framework for The Mailbox. The massive floor-loading capacity of the original building usefully accommodates significant loads in some parts of the office space, notably for the broadcasting facilities of the BBC. The housing at roof level is constructed from timber frames, pre-fabricated for delivery to site, and minimising additional loading.

The adaptation of the structural grid attunes the building's massive scale to its social and leisure uses. The shop fronts that infill the colonnades at ground- and first-floor levels modulate the users' experience. Metal angles frame the terracotta, and metal panels are used to cloak the floor edges, expressing their use as cladding rather than load-bearing elements.

Lighting

Lighting is used to reinforce the building's architectural qualities and give a dramatic presence by night. The principal elevations are uplit with white light to maintain a bright red image. The metal top of the building is illuminated with prismatic split light that focuses on this element. Internally the street columns are lit with focused up- and downlighting. Much of the character of the street is derived from light spill from the shop fronts, creating a variety of secondary effects in addition to the recessed lighting from the colonnades.

Regeneration and sustainability

The Mailbox is an exemplar of sustainability, bringing together a wide range of uses in intensive combination, and demonstrating that this juxtaposition of functions can be achieved. It harnesses and successfully adapts a massive concrete structure that would have been challenging and wasteful to demolish, doing justice to its embodied energy. In terms of thermal life cycle performance, it contributes by reducing the area of glazing and providing insulation to higher standards than those required by Building Regulations. A central cooling system supports the individual tenancies, using water from the adjacent canal basin as a heat dump to provide an energy-efficient solution, with capacity for the total anticipated building load.

The project is a strong example of integrated planning. It contributes to the successful regeneration of a large part of Birmingham as a major destination, close to major public transport facilities, and offering a high standard of pedestrian experience.

The Mailbox supports its retail tenants in projecting their own identities and appeal within a cohesive framework maintained by design guidelines. It is simple, elegant and legible, and functions as part of the city, offering a powerful alternative to more conventional indoor shopping malls that are typically overlit and cluttered. Whilst part of the development is under cover, it is essentially an arrangement of promenades open to the sky.

It is simple, elegant and legible, and functions as part of the city. Essentially an arrangement of promenades open to the sky, it offers a powerful alternative to more conventional indoor shopping malls.

ARCHITECTS
Associated Architects

CLIENT
Birmingham Mailbox Limited

PROJECT ADDRESS
Wharfside Street
Birmingham B1 1XL

AWARDS
Birmingham Civic Society Award, 2001
Estates Gazette Architecture Award, 2001
Finance Midlands Insider Property Awards, 2001 – Regeneration Award
Birmingham Design Initiative, 2002 – Urban Design Award
BURA Award for Waterways Renaissance, 2002
CABE High Quality Architecture Citation, 2002
British Council for Offices, Recycled Building Award, 2003 – Midlands Region
Civic Trust Award, 2003

↖ A low slung setting: dining and strolling along the waters' edge

↗ Two levels of retail stores and arcades, with the central promenade open to the sky

MERSEY VALLEY PROCESSING CENTRE

A sequence of articulated enclosures designed to house a necessary, but unwelcome, industrial plant. The thoughtfully configured composition signifies openness, reduces mass and accommodates the processing functions in discrete, well-resolved sculptural buildings in place of what might otherwise have been an intrusive, bulky box

The Mersey Valley Processing Centre is a cohesive group of buildings that house a sewage processing plant. The context is a sweeping valley, with wide vistas and residential accommodation close by. The project demonstrates the benefits that can be attained by approaching functional requirements from first principles, and successfully reducing scale and bulk. The solution addresses local sensitivity about the plant's function, location and scale by assimilating it in the landscape, and affording a degree of visual permeability that evokes a sense of openness about the activities undertaken inside.

The brief
The Mersey Valley Processing Centre is a regional sludge treatment facility located in Widnes, Merseyside. To the east is the large Fiddlers Ferry power station with its eight massive cooling towers and a domestic disposal plant. To the west is the residential area of Widnes.

The centre's function is to process treated liquid sewage sludge into 'cake' for recycling to agriculture and reclamation, and to incinerate surplus cake. The prospect of constructing the centre generated considerable sensitivity locally and regionally, both about the processes to be undertaken and the necessary scale of development. The resultant brief was for the centre to minimise its visual impact by limiting bulk, and to make a positive contribution by designing each element with care for its appearance and visual coherence between them.

To avoid a sense of concealment about the plant's processes, the buildings needed to be transparent about their purposes. The centre's close proximity to existing housing and offices reinforced the need for it to incorporate a high standard of design. The project was initiated in response to environmental legislation that required water companies to cease marine disposal of liquid sludge at the end of 1998, with disposal by incineration and recycling to agriculture and land reclamation instead. Due to the centre's nature and scale, a public inquiry was called, leaving 18 months between the planning consent and the date when the plant had to be operational. To achieve this, the design involved the frame and process plant being built and installed first, followed by the external skin, with features that did not contribute directly to this strategy eliminated. A generic design was modelled to optimise the plant configuration, both for the processing flow and to minimise the building footprints. Limiting the range of materials achieved economies of scale in procurement and an accelerated programme for construction.

↖ Roof over the incinerators, profiling the compacted volume of the centre's elegant enclosure

Overview

With 15,000 sq m gross area, the centre's minimum dimensions are determined by the nature and volume of the technical equipment it accommodates. This has resulted in a maximum building height of 30 m and a footprint of 200 m by 80 m.

The sequence of buildings relates to the processing activities. Four 3,200 cu m reception tanks house the arriving liquid sludge, and a large orthogonal box accommodates the 'dewatering' process. The office and control room are in a small square link building. Two large incinerators are located in one of two much larger, separate boxes – one for incineration, the other for odour treatment. The enclosure for the incinerators is covered by a single curved roof. An opening in this over-sailing roof allows for ash collection in an external space between the two boxes. There are two external stacks, a bank of four cooling towers, and a facility to store ash and load it onto vehicles in a sealed environment that avoids its dispersal during loading.

Little manpower is required for these processes: just 14 people routinely work on site by day and nine by night. A large office in the control block has an external deck providing alternative access to different parts of the plant, and a second large office with external aspect accommodates the other management staff. Controllers work in the control room, where the treatment process is tracked via an electronic mimic display panel. The remaining 'people space' comprises a kitchen, a meeting room and a flexible open-plan area for seminars and events. Every other built component is for plant. Every other person on site is a visitor – typically a truck driver or professional colleague.

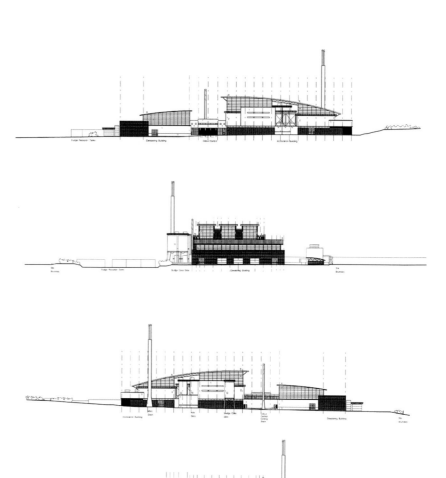

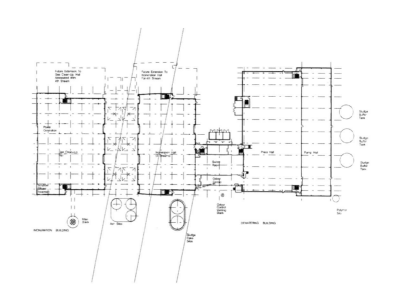

↗↗ Top set (from top down): north, east, south and west elevations

↗ Shell plan, ground floor

→ The plant in its Widnes Valley setting, with the Fiddlers Ferry power station to the left

What Mersey Valley Processing Centre shows

Breaking down bulk

At the necessary scale required by these industrial processes, the development could hardly be concealed. The strategy adopted was to reduce the centre's visual bulk by housing the distinct processes discretely, whilst giving visual coherence to these enclosures as a group. The outcome involves all the functions being housed in a series of elegant containers that cover the necessary processing equipment, without any being oversized.

Response to context

In contrast to being a blot in its setting, the centre provides a positive visual focus. The adjacent power station is huge and dominating, with an aesthetic of its own. The Mersey Valley plant is small by comparison and its elegance gives it strong visual appeal. The design has provided a cohesive complex of buildings that respond to the industrial setting in an authentic but refined manner. The variation in roof profile and the individuated block designs reduce the plant's overall mass on the skyline. This achievement is particularly beneficial in the wide valley setting, where a large box on the horizon would have been very prominent from a number of key viewpoints.

Articulating form; expressing function

The centre's appeal from a distance derives from the elegant profiles of its major elements – the blocks with their curved roofs, and the taller of the two stacks. The boxes' outlines correspond to the height and profiles of the plant within them, with the incinerators' curved roof significantly lowering the eaves height at the western end, compared to the 30 m height at its apex.

The elegance arises from the 'deconstructivist' strategy – treating the respective processes separately and enclosing them individually, in contrast to a more conventional approach – a single large box to house all the functions. A building with dimensions determined by the largest pieces or groups of plant would be massive and inevitably involve considerable wasted volume.

The design has provided a cohesive complex of buildings that respond to the industrial setting in an authentic but refined manner. The variation in roof profile and the individuated block designs reduce the plant's overall mass on the skyline.

Articulating the respective functions also offers expressive value, acknowledging what the plant is for. This is seen in the contoured profiles of the tanks, silos, cooling towers and stacks, the curved roofs of the blocks and the fluted roofs of the reception tanks. As well as indicating their purpose, these stand as sculptural elements in the landscape. The dynamic relationships between the elements as one alters one's vantage point make a further contribution.

Appropriate materials
From closer range, the plant's reassuring appearance also relates to its light and fresh materials palette. The selection emphasises the buildings' forms and reduces their visual impact from the middle distance, as well as providing for durability and low maintenance. The principal materials and textures are flat panel cladding, profile cladding, faced dense masonry and ribbed aluminium. The large buildings have a base of architectural masonry, with double-glazed low emissivity glass and heat-reflecting glazing at the lower and upper levels.

The rest of the cladding is in metal-faced composite panels – wide profile lower down the elevations, narrower profile higher up. Consistency across the buildings generates a well-edited sense of visual control.

The colours of the external materials are in the mid-tone range – mainly silver greys and warm greys, with buff-coloured masonry. These have a light, natural feel and set the buildings delicately in their surroundings where the light, reflective materials provide a refreshing contrast with the vast brown cooling towers of the adjacent power station.

Thinking through the design from first principles has resulted in a significant departure – functionally and aesthetically – from typical industrial space, enabling refinement in design.

←↑ Interior views, showing the scale of the plant that the enclosing structures house, with the large incinerator (right)

↗↗ Cohesive arrangement of structures, all tailored to the functional processes they support, and minimised in scale

↗ Crisp finish and sculptural form, projecting quality and confidence

The glazing provides numerous benefits, opening up views into the plant at the lower level and further relieving its visual bulk. The transparent planes humanise the centre for people who work there and demystify it for observers. The familiar vocabulary of windows promotes a sense of the plant as a safe place.

Benefits of first principles
The Mersey Valley Processing Centre involved delivery of a major technical infrastructure project and commissioning of plant on a tight programme. Thinking through the design from first principles has resulted in a significant departure – functionally and aesthetically – from typical industrial space, enabling refinement in design. Rather than a bland box or standard portal frame, redefining the accommodation as a series of elements, with rigour in the approach to their number, size and profile, has generated a composition of great clarity that contributes to its setting. Articulating the envelopes based on the respective functions that they house has been vital in achieving the project objective to limit visual bulk. It is open about the work done in the centre, imparting a strong sense of confidence and professionalism.

ARCHITECTS
Austin-Smith:Lord

CLIENT
North West Water

PROJECT ADDRESS
Dawson House
Great Sankey
Warrington WA5 3LW

AWARDS
British Construction Industry Major
    Project Award, 1999
RIBA Award, 1999

NEXUS

Designed for Orange as a centre for operational facilities and customer services, this building demonstrates excellent organisation, with a legible and stimulating sequence of spaces and scales, and a sense of unity throughout the arrangement

Providing comfortable accommodation and an attractive ambience for call-centre workers, Nexus has also been designed with inherent scope for conversion to an industrial shed. The building is distinguished by its internal organisation, rational layout and clear spatial arrangement. The envelope encloses a single large volume, modulated to provide a range of interior settings and scales, from spaces for individuals and small groups, to two large areas each accommodating over two hundred people in a single visual field. The building benefits from innovative lighting design, both natural and artificial. A double-height central support spine, dramatic uplighters and imaginative meeting enclosures contribute to a high level of animation and strong sense of place, based on a durable aesthetic.

The brief

The Nexus building, on an industrial site in Darlington, was commissioned for use as a call centre. Designed to accommodate 440 workstations, it had to be spatially efficient, whilst comfortable and inspiring for the people who work there. To provide institutional value in the context of its site, it needed to be capable of easy conversion to an industrial or warehouse use.

The envelope was to be a lean structure of simple construction, with the budget concentrated on the interior and the focus on facilitating the operational activities and supporting and stimulating the employees. The objective was for an open, bright, fresh space, with the requisite facilities in easy reach by people working in the building as well as those from other Orange buildings on the site. A data centre with its associated requirement for security formed part of the brief.

↖ Comfort and legibility: desk area with the ribbon window, circular ETFE foil rooflights and dramatic lighting trees, edged by timber and glass meeting pods

Overview

The building provides 4,870 sq m net area in a 9 m high volume. The ground floor is divided into two equal open-plan zones, each accommodating 220 workstations, with the full sectional height above. In plan and section, the building is bisected by a two-storey central support spine incorporating the computer centre, WCs and conference rooms at ground level, and the restaurant, coffee bar and kitchen above.

The envelope is a largely pre-fabricated structure, in lightweight material. The south-facing, fully glazed, 60 m front elevation announces the building on the site, admits natural light to the interior, offers the employees views out, and provides a distinctive illuminated plane when the call centre is in operation after dark. This is externally shaded by high-level louver sunshades and internally by automatic roll-down blinds.

The steel roof structure uses continuous beams. Haunches are eliminated and the traditional universal beam legs replaced by circular columns. The roof beams support a deep-profiled metal decking, perforated for improved acoustic performance. The metal decking is designed as a stressed skin diaphragm, bracing the building and distributing the wind loads to vertical braced frames. Bracing for the glazed front elevation is incorporated into the structure for the central spine.

The lighting is thoughtful and innovative. A 72 m long, 1,200 mm high ribbon window along both sides and the rear elevation gives all round external awareness without glare. Ten 6 m circular ETFE foil rooflights diffuse natural light from above, and feature luminaires on tall circular columns provide diffused uplight through their distinctive fabric petals.

Delivered at a high level in the space, this solution achieves an average lighting level of 350 lux at the desks, meeting the preferred performance standard for call-centre activity set by the brief. The lighting control is coordinated with the BMS (building management system), enabling full use of natural lighting.

An underfloor air distribution system supplies conditioned fresh air via floor-mounted swirl-type diffusers. Supplied at this low level, slightly below the room temperature, the air rises through natural buoyancy as it is heated by the occupants and the activities in the building, before it is extracted at high level with mechanical assistance. The solution provides a fresh environment and constant temperature whilst being energy efficient.

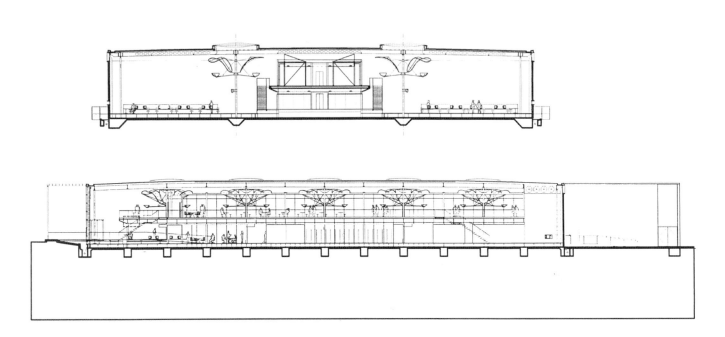

↑↑ Cross-section, showing the centre's symmetrical arrangement, with an operational floor on either side of the central spine

↑ Long section, showing the procession of lighting trees down the centre's length

↗ Plans: ground floor with meeting pods on either side of the central spine (left), upper floor of the central spine accommodating the kitchen, restaurant, coffee bar and galleried walkways (right)

What Nexus shows

Flexibility as sustainable design

The building's design for flexibility is instructive. Given the major shifts in the nature of employment based on computer and communications technology, questions over the viability of whole sectors of activity are inherent. The scope for Nexus to convert to industrial accommodation following a possible future reduction in call-centre operations exemplifies a sustainable approach. Within this framework, the priority given to users' experience is appropriate to the building's current function. Nexus demonstrates good integration of the envelope and fit-out design, with both playing key roles.

Supportive spatial organisation

Nexus is exemplary in its approach to spatial organisation, layering the building users' experience both by activity and the size of groupings involved. Accommodating 440 people in an orthogonal structure at a density of one workstation per 5.5 sq m could be a crude affair. Indeed, even in some call processing centres with smaller floor plates, differentiation and ordering of spatial experience is often lacking. In contrast, Nexus provides a sequence in its spatial arrangement that is highly legible, functionally effective and visually stimulating. The layout clearly reveals the building's component settings from all internal positions, giving users a sense of connection to the wider organisation throughout the course of their activities.

Functional expression

The two large open areas, operating as distinct zones on either side of the shared central spine, are mirror images of one another. The routes connecting these zones pass through the base of the spine. Interactive activities are accommodated on the perimeter of both zones. These meeting spaces define the edges of the operational area, contain it and limit disruption to individuals' work. Space for small private conversations by two or three people is provided in semi-enclosed cubicles that face the building's front elevation. Larger meeting 'pods' are aligned with the service spine. Large conference rooms are incorporated in the base of the spine, on the ground floor. The hierarchy of settings – from individual to communal – is expressed in terms of spatial proximity to the desk area, with the most interactive settings furthest away.

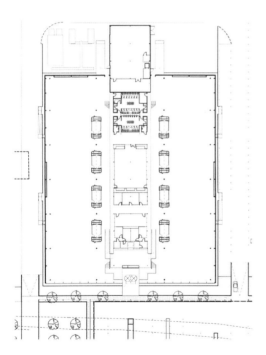 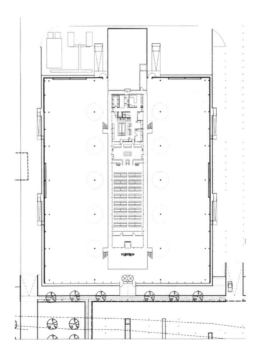

Nexus provides a sequence in its spatial arrangement that is highly legible, functionally effective and visually stimulating.

Contrasting functions are accommodated on different levels: work activity is on the ground floor and refreshment and relaxation on the upper level of the support spine. The elevated restaurant and coffee bar are visible from the workstations as beacons of a break from work activity. Given the large element of repetitive work activity in call centres, this expression of contrast is beneficial.

The upper level is reached via an exposed staircase on each side of the spine. Horizontal circulation on the upper level is on open galleries that run the length of the mezzanine on each side. As people seated at their desks observe movement along these routes, the arrangement contributes to the building's animation. The reverse view, from the stairs and galleries, encompasses an entire zone of the operational space, promoting the viewer's comprehension of the centre's organisation and settings. This affords a valuable sense of connection to the enterprise beyond each employee's individual role.

From the upper level, the benefits of dividing the operational area into two are readily apparent. Zones for 200 rather than 400 workers reduce the distance they need to cover between their desks and the interactive spaces. Larger zones would also be superfluous for management purposes and counter-productive socially. As it is, the scale is significant and the arrangement capitalises on its drama, without sacrificing individuals' comfort by accommodating them in a spatial field that is larger than necessary.

The arrangement capitalises on the drama of the building's arrangement without sacrificing individuals' comfort and sense of place.

↖ Staircase to upper level from the entrance foyer area

← Semi-enclosed areas for meetings of two or three people at the edge of the desk area, facing the glazed front elevation

↗ View from the desk area to the upper level walkway and restaurant, mediated by the timber and glass meeting pods between the desk area and the two-storey spine

↗↗ Meeting pods: balancing a sense of openness and containment in the large operational area

Look, feel and sense of place

The sense of drama is heightened by the visual impact of the light diffusers on the distinctive 'service trees'. Their curved petals have a sculptural quality, as do the circular rooflights. These features provide a strong counterpoint to the orthogonal elements in the design: the envelope, mezzanine spine structure, ground-floor layout, workstation furniture and meeting venues.

Colour is introduced in an integral way. The desks are separated from one another by low partition screens, coloured in three discrete bands graduating from dark to light orange and then to yellow, from the front to the rear of the floor. Colour is also used to advantage in the decorative text applied to the glazing that encloses the meeting pods.

These distinctive, part-glazed, part-timber, open-topped settings display colourful graphics based on the theme of communication, signifying both to the organisation's business and the function served by the pods. Individually and collectively these features contribute to the strong sense of place inside the Nexus building.

ARCHITECTS
Grimshaw

CLIENT
Orange PCS

PROJECT ADDRESS
Orange Operational Facilities and
Customer Services Centre
Nexus House
Senhouse Road
Darlington DL1 4YQ

AWARDS
RIBA Award, 1999 – Regional Award
Structural Steel Design Awards, 1999
    Commendation

NORTH GREENWICH UNDERGROUND STATION

Built entirely below ground level, the station's organisation and imaginative use of materials provide a sense of spaciousness, good orientation and a rich experience of light and colour

Natural light and views to the outside are highly valued by building users. Optimising daylight and external aspect in building interiors is now a hallmark of effective design. Where the site precludes this, the challenge is not only to evoke a comparable experience inside the building, but to avoid a sense of claustrophobia and promote orientation without reliance on external vistas as an aid. As a completely subterranean building, North Greenwich Underground Station responds to an extreme version of these demands. It not only involves a highly constrained site, but its position fully underground makes it unique in the sequence of stations on the Jubilee Line Extension and gives it exceptional conditions to meet. North Greenwich Underground Station demonstrates how the standards of clarity and legibility now associated with its peer group buildings can be achieved in other ways. The design offers a rich user experience through creative spatial arrangements and a masterful selection of materials.

The brief

North Greenwich Underground Station is located at the tip of the Greenwich Peninsula. As the site formerly accommodated Europe's largest gasworks, large quantities of contaminated soil had to be removed to enable its construction.

The station was designed to serve the Millennium Village and other developments on the Greenwich Peninsula – both those existing at the time and others that were expected to follow. The client sought to retain the land above the station to develop further buildings.

The underground station is approached through a new bus station (designed by another firm), with the two stations forming a transport interchange. From a passenger's vantage point, the two are fluently integrated: the escalators leading down to the underground station are entered at ground level inside the bus station.

The overall objectives set for the building were a sense of openness and clarity for passengers and simplicity of function for operations. With the high level of user comfort sought for all the stations on the Jubilee Line Extension, its site conditions set a particular design challenge for the North Greenwich Station. A good user experience needed to be facilitated without lighting the space excessively, and using lighting solutions based on the standard fittings for all stations on the extended line. The design also needed to enable easy maintenance.

↖ Clear visual connections from platform level to the concourse and underside of the station's lid, promoting a sense of spaciousness and orientation

Overview

Although the largest station on the Jubilee Line, capable of handling around 20,000 passengers an hour, North Greenwich Underground Station is externally visible only by its entrance and ventilation shafts. The client's requirement that the land at ground level be kept free for subsequent 'air rights' development determined a 'cut and cover' approach. The entire station is built below ground level and enclosed by a 'lid', supported by 21 pairs of columns, cast in situ, with each pair angled in a V formation. Below the lid, the ground was excavated to create a long rectangular box – 360 m long, 30 m wide and 13 m deep. This accommodates three tracks, enabling provision for through traffic as well as terminating trains and a potential branch into south London.

On entering the station, passengers step onto escalators and immediately descend to a concourse below ground level. There is also lift access between the ground and concourse levels. The concourse, suspended from the station lid by 80 mm diagonal solid steel tie rods with a stainless steel finish and 48 hour fire protection, is essentially a bridge that runs centrally down the station's visible length. The ticketing facilities are located at the nearest point of arrival on the concourse, close to the base of the escalators to the west. Low-level vertical glass panels on either side of the concourse provide edge protection and views to the platforms below. Full-height voids between the concourse edges and the walls that enclose the far edges of the outer platforms rise from the platform level below.

The platforms are reached via escalators from both sides of the concourse, again with alternative access by lift. The three tracks are aligned east–west, slightly asymmetrically relative to the concourse. Glazed screens at the platform edges form a barrier to the tracks.

The concourse structure contains the station's services, and its base incorporates a void for access by maintenance staff. A cantilevered steel scissors stair is suspended on diagonal hollow steel tubes between the concourse and the platform, providing maintenance access to the escalator machine rooms that are suspended above the platforms.

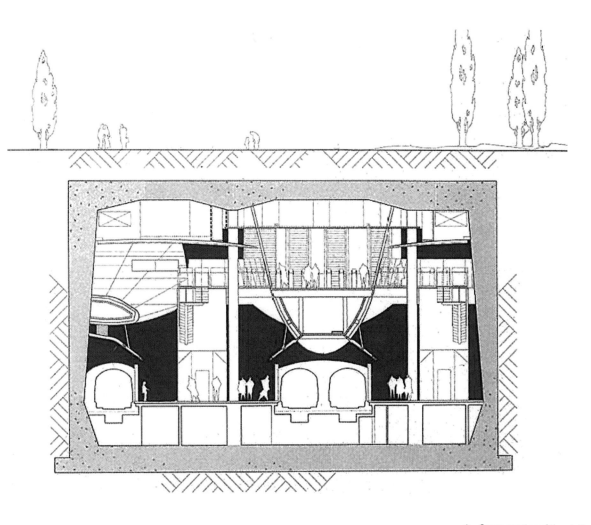

↑   Cross-section of the station, showing the asymmetrical platform arrangement and suspended concourse with access space for servicing beneath

→   Concept sketches

What North Greenwich Underground Station shows

Clear orientation and ease of movement

The station's design is substantially determined by the alignment of the tracks and the platform length, making the building's proportions inherently linear. Despite its confinement to underground space with no daylight penetration, and with the stringent operational requirements relating to rail service, North Greenwich Underground Station is easy to use and clear to negotiate. The absence of external views from within the building, combined with the constrained space and lack of natural light, required the design to deploy other measures to promote orientation in the station. This has been achieved by skilful spatial organisation, use of form and selection of surface treatments. The result is a sympathetic and comfortable user environment that offers visual stimulus and effective cues to ease movement through the station.

Most users of transport buildings are passengers, but maintenance workers are another key user constituency. Ease of maintenance is central to safety as well as sustainability. The design provides for low-maintenance finishes where possible, and shows innovation in providing safe access for maintenance to high-level areas.

Sense of spaciousness

The expansive feel inside the station derives from the building's organisation. Clear space on either side of the concourse increases the perceived width of the interior that might otherwise have felt unduly restrictive. This perception is enhanced by the use of dark blue glass across the full height of the side wall, increasing visual depth in the space. Exposing the station's full internal height from the platform level to the underside of the station lid facilitates visual connections across levels, further enhancing the sense of spaciousness, promoting orientation and making the journey through the building legible.

Suspending the escalator machine rooms makes yet another contribution, liberating space on the central platform for passenger movement and visual amenity.

Colour, texture and form

One's experience inside the station is greatly enriched by the use of colour. The walls, floors and ceilings involve a range of materials coloured an intense blue. This generates an exciting ambience and gives the station a coherent character and identity.

The V-shaped columns have a strong sculptural impact. Their massive presence is counter-pointed by the myriad small tiles that cover them. This blue glass mosaic tile cladding has a reflective effect that reinforces the columns' angled form and the grandeur of their procession down the station's length.

The absence of external views from within the building, combined with the constrained space and lack of natural light, required the design to deploy other measures to promote orientation in the station. This has been achieved by spatial organisation, use of form and surface treatments.

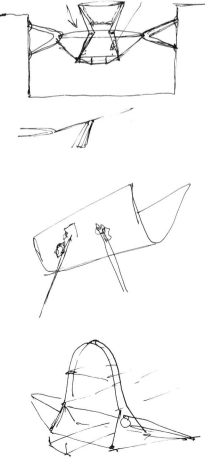

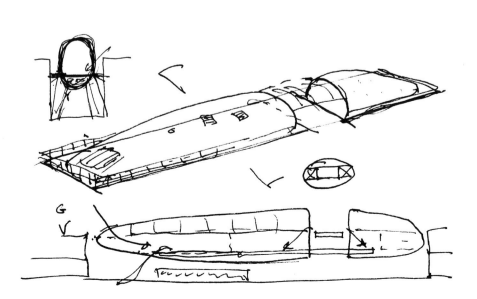

As these structures rise through the full height of the void and frame the edges of the suspended concourse at rhythmic intervals, they provide a consistent point of reference that allows passengers to read the space horizontally and vertically. The columns' visual texture is further enhanced by small insets of red mosaic.

The blue theme is continued in the rich glass wall that borders the south platform. This is back-lit, giving the impression of blue light. The blue and red tile combination is repeated in a tailored motif on the glazed barriers on the upper concourse, and the blue tiles are also used to face the walls that flank the entrance escalators and ticketing hall. On both the platform and concourse levels, the use of strong colour is complemented by the floor – predominantly white terrazzo textured with blue and red particles.

One's experience inside the station is greatly enriched by the use of colour. The walls, floors and ceilings involve a range of materials coloured an intense blue. This generates an exciting ambience and gives the station a coherent character and identity.

↖ Views at platform level, with the predominantly white floor complementing the intense blue of the vertical surfaces (top and bottom)

Views of the concourse:
↗↗ The ticket hall and sense of connection afforded by the distinctive columns that pass down the void on either side
↗ Bowed ceiling ribs under the lid combining with the vertical columns to envoke the subtle image of a ship

Sense of place

Overall the architects have created
an efficient, legible station with a
distinctive sense of place. The building
demonstrates the vitality, interest and
sense of order that can be created entirely
below ground level by good spatial
arrangement, exploiting the scale and
drama of the engineering elements, and
intelligent use of colour and materials.
The lighting, using the standard fixtures
permitted, is a notable achievement; the
result is well balanced and stimulating
without being too brightly lit.

The station's organisation and form, the
multiplicity of vertical elements – columns
and concourse structure, as well as the
bowed ceiling ribs under the lid – all
evoke a subtle image of a ship with its
rigging. This gesture to a maritime theme
is strengthened by the prominence of blue
internal cladding. The reference offers
a useful symbolic link to the Greenwich
Peninsula, the more so as there is
no direct visual connection with the
surroundings.

ARCHITECTS
SMC Alsop Architects
    (formerly Alsop and Störmer)
Project initiated by Alsop Lyall and
    Störmer

CLIENT
Jubilee Line Extension Ltd

PROJECT ADDRESS
5 Millennium Way
London SE10 0PH

AWARDS
RIBA Civic and Community Award,
    1999
Royal Fine Art Commission's
    Millennium Buildings of the Year
    Award to Jubilee Line Extension,
    2000 – Special Commendation

OXO TOWER RESTAURANT

A recycled building accommodating a combination of privileged social and public uses, and incorporating a new top floor with dynamic restaurant spaces that exploit the waterfront site's panoramas and extend the high-level views of London to a wide range of users

The Oxo Tower Restaurant harnesses the opportunity offered by a Thameside site facing the City of London to celebrate the views from this exciting location. The project vision entailed the adaptation of an old warehouse building to a mix of uses centred on social housing, craft workshops and studios, and topped by a fine restaurant and public viewing platform. The project demonstrates that this array of uses and users is not only feasible, but can be complementary. It shows the role of intelligent spatial configuration and elegant design in generating and maintaining the restaurant's appeal, and hence the necessary value for this project, with its significant social benefits, to succeed.

The brief

The mixed-use Oxo Tower Wharf redevelopment has been a fulcrum in the regeneration of London's South Bank. The 1,200 sq m restaurant, bar and brasserie is a significant component in this achievement.

The project involved the redevelopment of a meat warehouse that had been created by recycling a post office power station originally constructed in 1908. Its former conversion to the meat store saw the addition of its art deco tower, with the iconic apertures spelling OXO.

The recent case study project comprised several parts. The warehouse was gutted to its reinforced concrete frame and new accommodation provided: shops, cafés and design workshops on the two lower levels, a food court and over 30 further design workshops on the second floor, and five floors with 78 flats above. The restaurant is on a new ninth floor, constructed on top of the building especially for this purpose.

The architects were first appointed by Coin Street Community Builders on the overall building project, to design the other uses and the restaurant shell. The original red brick elevations were restored, and steel and timber balconies added to the waterfront elevation. The south elevation was reconstructed in a simple modern manner that accords with the retained façades. Three new cores were constructed – the main core below the tower, and the secondary cores as brick towers at the building's east and west ends.

The restaurateur's brief was to create a bustling, vibrant brasserie and a more formal restaurant, both capitalising on the site's wonderful views. The client considered it an advantage that the architects had not designed a restaurant previously, coming to the project without preconceived ideas, thus enabling the design boundaries to be pushed. A fundamental client requirement was for an architectural solution to provide for controlled change in the restaurant's ambience by day and night.

↖ Dining by night, inside and on the terrace, with the romantic hue from the aerofoil fins in their blue night-time position

Overview

The linear restaurant space, with its 80 m by 18 m footprint, sits neatly on the building's rectangular plan. Accommodating a more formal restaurant in one half and a more relaxed brasserie in the other, the basic space for both is similar, with their difference in character based on fit-out elements – the design of the bars and the selection and density of the loose furniture.

The ninth-floor space is double volume, below a new lightweight monopitch roof that slopes upwards to the waterfront elevation. Both the long elevations are fully glazed. The glass wall on the riverside is 6 m high and slopes outward towards the roof. A 33 m wide external terrace runs along the full building length. The central core, containing the lifts, WCs and the facilities to run the restaurant – kitchen, reception desks, coat storage – is set back from the elevations, leaving free space at the floor plate edge for horizontal circulation and from which users can enjoy the views.

Steel trusses that support the roof at 4.5 m centres are set on paired slender steel columns along the centre of the building. The roof is constructed from profiled aluminium sheeting, laid in single lengths over the full span. It has a perforated liner tray with dense mineral fibre slabs as an acoustic absorber, and a structural deck to resist racking of the roof trusses.

The cantilevered aerofoil ceiling above the dining areas incorporates motorised double-sided rotating fins that provide acoustic control, as well as the controlled variation of interior look and feel required by the client. This provides a pristine pale finish for a light and airy ambience by day, and an ultramarine surface that promotes a romantic mood at night. An additional floating floor provides acoustic insulation.

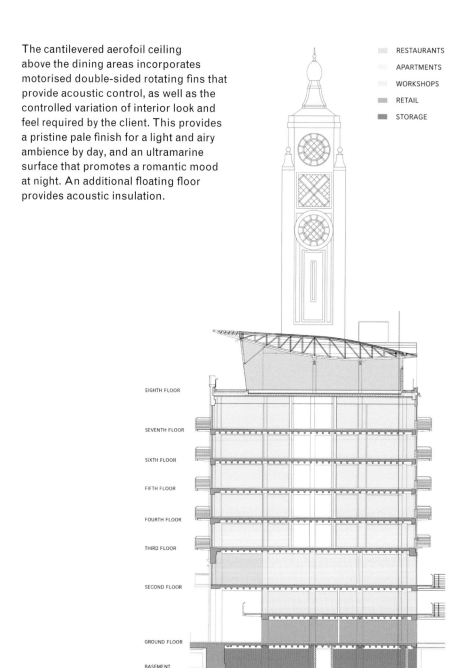

RESTAURANTS
APARTMENTS
WORKSHOPS
RETAIL
STORAGE

EIGHTH FLOOR

SEVENTH FLOOR

SIXTH FLOOR

FIFTH FLOOR

FOURTH FLOOR

THIRD FLOOR

SECOND FLOOR

GROUND FLOOR

BASEMENT

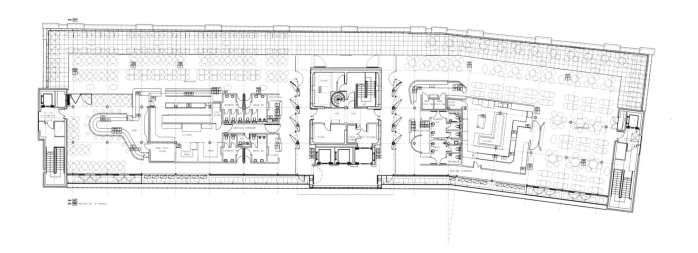

What Oxo Tower Restaurant shows

Social sustainability and sense of place

The Oxo Tower Restaurant exemplifies sustainable practice in several important ways. Its re-use of an existing building structure (with this project constituting its second major functional adaptation) encompasses a responsible approach to embodied energy. The design is also effective in articulating and sustaining the social memory of this part of London, by retaining the warehouse building's form and reinforcing its signature Oxo lantern. The restaurant's location on top of the building signifies it externally. Its soaring front elevation below the deco tower announces the building as a contemporary venue. This horizontal band provides the building with a light and airy lid by day, whilst at night the lit elevation, accentuated by the blue hue from its aerofoil ceiling, expresses the building's life. The project's success in 'place-making' has made the building a destination and contributed to regeneration in the locality.

The restaurant also promotes a wider appreciation of London. The site offers inherent potential for magnificent views – northwards to the opposite river bank with St Pauls Cathedral, the financial buildings of the City, the law courts, Somerset House, Old Scotland Yard, the Palace of Westminster, and the West End and vast cityscape beyond, as well as panoramic views across south London. The restaurant design exploits its capacity to promote enjoyment of these views.

The most obvious device is the long terrace on the riverside. As part of the base building design, the original parapet on this elevation was lowered by one metre to facilitate views from the restaurant. The location of the core and enclosed service elements 'inboard' on the floor is also key. This leaves the perimeter space on both long elevations free of obstructions, enabling uninterrupted aspect through the glazing. The column-free façade design with the frameless glazing suspended from the roof structure heightens the marvellous sense of feeling connected to all of London. Though most of the terrace area is given to use by patrons of the restaurant and brasserie, a valuable social benefit is the building owner's stipulation that anyone can access the ninth-level terrace just to enjoy the views.

Facilitating complementary uses

The specific mix at Oxo Tower is visionary in its combination of functions and users. The large restaurant is pivotal in this blend, creating the value that has facilitated the design, construction and maintenance of the building's other uses at the high standard that has been achieved. The mix of uses stems from an audacious vision and is supported by effective protocols for use, but design plays a critical role, with important provisions to facilitate the mix.

These include the configuration of the central core with a dedicated lift to the restaurant, the segregated restaurant services, the design of the slab between the restaurant floor and the flats below, and the insertion of an acoustic floor above this. This underpins sustainable co-existence between the restaurant clientele as they come and go and the residential tenants on the levels below.

Creating value through design appeal

The restaurant's success also depends on it being a 'great space'. The venue needed to attract and retain an operator who could make the financial values work, and continue to attract custom through the term of the lease. This needed to be achieved through design, with the influence of the design weightier than in a typical project, because the location was just nascent as a new cultural quarter when the project was conceived, and the potential for a large restaurant here had yet to be established. The design has delivered on its promise. It complements the views afforded by the setting, playing a strong part in attracting the level of custom that the setting alone could not ensure.

The mix of uses stems from an audacious vision and is supported by effective protocols for use, but design plays a critical role, with important provisions to facilitate the mix.

↖ Short section of Oxo Tower building, showing the mix of uses

← Plan of Oxo Tower Restaurant, with the restaurant (to the right) and the brasserie (to the left), on either side of the central core, positioned to leave both the south-facing elevation and the waterfront elevation and terraces with unobstructed panoramic views

→ The Oxo Tower building from the south-west, showing the new ninth floor that accommodates the Oxo Tower Restaurant, and the two new 'bookend cores'

Staged arrival

A number of decisions contribute to the design's success. One is bringing guests to a point of arrival on entering the restaurant, in the relatively narrow space between the central core and the southward elevation. This welcome post at the midpoint on the linear floor plate poises patrons for the dramatic opening up of the space that they then experience as they are led into the restaurant or brasserie. In part, the appeal of these spaces is associated with their spatial scale. The architects have planned an exciting sequence of arrival.

Spatial experience

Whilst both the long elevations offer panoramic views, the inclined glazed façade on the riverside plays an additional role. Hanging from the roof, this high glass wall extends the vista that it offers beyond the panoramic strip of London's north bank – it also incorporates the sky.

The effect is significant in making the restaurant feel expansive, and in re-shaping the internal spatial experience from the linear format based on the floor plate to one that soars up and outward through the lofty glazed elevation. This sense of soaring height is facilitated by the cantilevered roof.

Look and feel

Numerous design features contribute to the restaurant's appeal as an attractive place. The motorised ceiling with its aerofoil fins effects changes in surface colour, acoustics, texture and lighting. It also works in combination with the sloping north elevation to eliminate internal reflections that would obstruct views out from the restaurant at night. The rotating fins have an additional function in providing for acoustic variability, with the opening and closing of the louvers allowing for variation in reverberation times. Their alternating surface finishes are used to change the restaurant ambience at different times of day and night. Lighting variation is achieved by control of the intensity and colour from the ambient downlighting and the fluorescent lighting behind the rotating fins. The fins' variable positions provide for variations in light colour and exposure.

The interior of the Oxo Tower Restaurant has presence as a stylish, quietly stated, generously scaled space, offering a strong base from which to appreciate the large ceiling plane with its distinctive aerofoil fins and the dramatic external view. The simple finishes – light timber on the floors and white walls – provide a neutral backdrop for the loose furniture.

Rounded achievement

The conception and design of the Oxo Tower restaurant have intelligently exploited the opportunity offered by the site, creating a desirable venue and demonstrating the feasibility of mixed use. It demonstrates the role of good design in generating value and facilitating a combination of uses that yields wide benefits, including renewed vitality to its setting.

↖ Spectacular panorama, facing the City of London, with the restaurant's aerofoil fins in position for daytime ambience

← Being 'in the sky', coupled with more panorama – from this vantage point, to London's West End

↗ The signature blue light from the aerofoil fins, further enhancing the Oxo Tower Restaurant's contribution atop the lively mix of building uses facing the river

ARCHITECTS
Lifschutz Davidson Sandilands

CLIENT
Coin Street Community Builders (base build)
Harvey Nichols Restaurants Ltd (fit-out)

PROJECT ADDRESS
Oxo Tower Wharf
Barge House Street
London SE1 9PH

AWARDS
Oxo Tower Bar, Restaurant
RIBA Award, 1997

Oxo Tower Wharf
Brick Development Association Award, 1997
RIBA Award, 1997
Royal Fine Arts Commission, 1997 – Urban Regeneration Award
Civic Trust Award, 1998
The Waterfront Centre USA, 2000 – Honour Award

PENTLAND LAKESIDE

Fine workspace and staff amenities inside and out in a timeless building that affords rich stimulus whilst sitting discreetly in its residential context

This headquarters project demonstrates a new approach to workplace design – located close to living environments, but without the lack of design vision typical of suburban development. Design is central to Pentland's business and the building is highly effective in expressing this. Its internal environment and integration with its external landscaped setting have a timeless quality. At the same time the interior space facilitates the conception and display of the more ephemeral fashion cycles that the building serves to promote.

The brief

Pentland is an international brand management company owning and holding licences for branded sports, outdoor and fashion items, and supplying clothing and footwear to retailers. Active worldwide, Pentland is headquartered in North London.

In the mid-1990s the company decided to expand onto the site adjacent to its existing premises, centralising most of its UK operations on a single campus, with a new building to accommodate its administrative, marketing, executive and design teams. The challenge of attracting talent to this location, and retaining it, in competition with the employment opportunities amidst the cosmopolitan buzz of central London, set the building brief. Pentland wanted a building that provided a high-quality workplace, defined a leading standard for working environments and rivalled central London accommodation. The building was to be exciting and stimulating, whilst providing a 'family' environment.

A particular requirement was to house labels that are potential competitors in an open and uplifting building, without compromising the security of the respective brands' intellectual property. The architects worked closely with Pentland's marketing department and the individual brands, establishing user groups and a design committee to help achieve a solution that satisfied the range of needs and aspirations.

After extensive consultation in the neighbouring residential areas, related design development and the receipt of planning consent, the original proposal was scaled down and an iterated scheme completed in 2002.

↖ Outdoors and in: enjoying lunch on the waterside deck from the restaurant behind the terrace

Overview

The 9,448 sq m gross building is arranged as three distinct elements, with four floors housing 5,400 sq m of working area, and two floors of communal space totalling 4,048 sq m. The entrance block is a generous, double-volume main foyer and reception area, on a large faceted triangular plan of 30 m by 30 m by 42 m, rising to 7 m under a copper roof that slopes downward towards the arrival route. The foyer leads into a 16.5 m by 16.5 m low pavilion that accommodates a restaurant, breakfast bar and kitchen. Both these blocks are glass clad with a steel structure. The main work areas are in a five-storey 'office block', recessed in a sharply banked site and comprising two 60 m long floor plates separated by a linear atrium. Incorporating design and marketing studios, office space, meeting and presentation rooms, club space, gym and dance studio, steam rooms, changing facilities and a showroom, this block has a slab and concrete structure on a 7.5 m grid, giving the floor plates 15 m spans. The external skin is yellow facing brickwork. A fourth significant element is a covered bridge across the lake, linking the building to a (now refurbished) 1960s office building that was developed by the former site owner and is also used by Pentland.

What Pentland Lakeside shows

Timeless container; high fashion inside
Aptly for a company that deals in fashion and brand identity, the Pentland building is full of wit and visual interest. The numerous zones and spaces have names referencing the previous site owner, the Electricity Generating Board: 'Mainfeed' – the restaurant, 'Circuit' – the gym, 'Meltdown' – the relaxation zone, 'Sparks' – the internet café and 'Source' – the retail showcase.

Many features, including lighting, furniture, artworks and pieces commissioned by Pentland from award-winning students, exude design flair. None of the interior settings is mundane. For example, the 'Glass Lake' is a steel sculpture of a figure diving into a lake of glass that forms an exterior square framed by the foyer's glazed rear elevation. The 'Testimonial Wall' is a light box that displays multi-lingual 'text bites' conveying Pentland's business approach along the full length of the long atrium.

The pictorial 'History Wall', showcasing Pentland's history from its inception as the Liverpool Shoe Company in 1932 to the brand management group it is today, runs the length of the minor atrium that is aligned north–south between the foyer and office blocks.

Whilst many buildings that are focused on fashion concentrate all their expression on the excitement that this sector offers, the Pentland building is vivacious without condescension. In part this derives from its materials – brick, slate, copper, timber, expressed steel, glass and aluminium. The plant areas have a sedum roof, and copper is prominent on both the building and the bridge over the lake. The external timber decking is highly integrated with both the building and its setting in one's experience of the space.

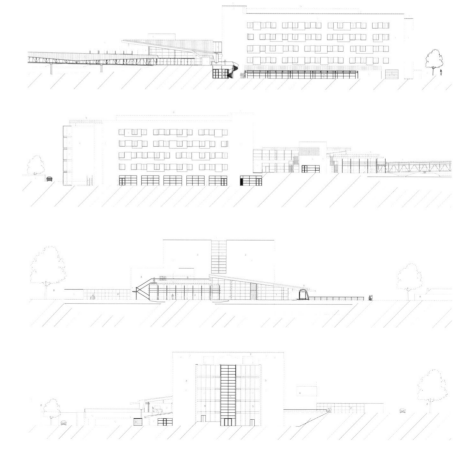

→ Elevations (top to bottom): front and bridge; from the rear courtyard; from the lake – restaurant, reception and office blocks; from the car park, facing north east

→→ Plans across the steeply banked site (top to bottom): lower ground – the office block; the entrance level, with restaurant, reception area and office block; and typical upper floor

The balance of punch and enduring design is well demonstrated in the reception area, where the natural feel is conveyed by the use of timber and glass. The expansive foyer accommodates significant accent elements such as large plasma screens, a moving conveyor belt that displays products from Pentland's brand selection, a 15 m by 3 m glass walkway and the backlit reception desk. The brick south elevation of the office block, seen through the foyer's glazed roof slot, further expands the palette of materials that enriches the foyer area. It also provides a sense of enclosure in this extensively glazed space, and intimates a seriousness of purpose.

The abiding characteristic of the foyer space is its spatial quality, an environment at once uplifting and comfortable, where one can marvel at the 'toys', meet informally, relax or work on-line.

The building is exemplary in its parallel focus on fashion and enduring design. The life cycle inherent in each of these is different. Fashion is fast, good buildings are more timeless and robust. Pentland Lakeside succeeds in reconciling this difference.

Interface with exterior

The key public areas flow visually one to another. The foyer – with its external triangular plan form and monopitch copper canopy that spans 20 m over the space and engages with the lake – flows to the restaurant. The floor-to-ceiling glazing affords south-, west- and east-facing panoramic views onto the water. From both the foyer and restaurant spaces there is a seamless view to the surrounding external deck. With its glazed cladding and extensive use of natural materials that blur the distinction between inside and out, the deck feels like an outward extension of the indoor space.

The rich materials, including fair-faced concrete exposed columns, brickwork, slate and flooring of pebbles set in resin, form a grounded 'organic' counterpoint to the entertaining array of interior features. The visual focus provided by the lake is a coup, repaying the investment in the landscape that surrounds it and the decision to enhance this formerly contaminated body of water, bringing the oasis that it now is to conservation standards. The roof of the restaurant block is safely accessible and used for staff events and product launches, further integrating the building and its immediate setting.

Effective, tolerant workspace

The Pentland building is also about work! Above the ground floor, the main block has four levels that can be flexibly deployed as studio space for the brands, and as office space for the group marketing, legal, HR and management teams. This space sits symmetrically on either side of the atrium that brings natural light and ventilation into the deeper zones. Several design decisions serve to enhance the perceived width of the atrium that is just 5.5 m. The main circulation routes are aligned with the atrium edge, the wire balustrades along the atrium edges promote visual expansion of the volume into the floor plates on either side, and much of the workspace is free of high partitions and entirely open to the atrium. The arrangement also increases the perceived floor-to-ceiling height on the office floors beyond their actual dimension.

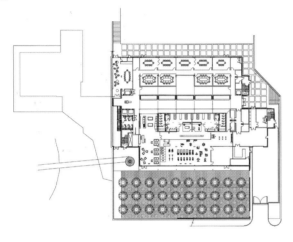

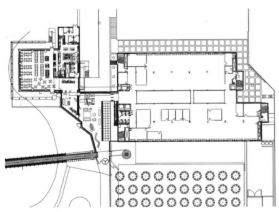

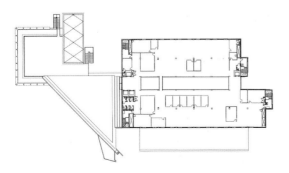

The building is exemplary in its parallel focus on fashion and enduring design. The life cycle inherent in each of these is different. Fashion is fast, good buildings are more timeless and robust. Pentland Lakeside succeeds in reconciling this difference.

↑↑ Capitalising on the site's potential: the glazed restaurant block surrounded by outdoor decking overlooks the lake now brought to conservation standard

↑ Bridge connecting to an existing office building on the site, with copper cover relating to the eaves on the restaurant and reception pavilions, and the office block with yellow facing brickwork

← Secondary atrium between the reception and office blocks, with the long expanse harnessed as a 'history wall'

Overall, the space is well unified, with the two wings linked across the atrium by bridges at both ends of all the floors, and by a series of bridges at intervals along the atrium length. All the office floors overlook the street on the atrium base below, where the resin-bonded gravel walkway doubles as a catwalk for shows and product launches.

In contrast to the visually permeable foyer and restaurant blocks, the office space is far more enclosed. Its brick elevations and lower ratio of glazing provide 80 per cent opacity, affording privacy and working conditions in which staff can concentrate without excessive external distraction, as well as facilitating reduced energy use. The approach was for a modest, tolerant building. Although the office space is fitted with fan-coil air-conditioning, it is designed to operate in a mixed-mode system using natural ventilation, and the foyer and restaurant blocks operate on a displacement system. The louvers on the south-facing office wall and restaurant, and the deep canopy overhanging the glazed elevations offer further protection against solar gain.

The facilities are all well designed to support their functions. The internal space is a combination of glazed offices and open plan work areas, with internal partitioning where required to provide privacy for brands that may be in competition. There are formal and informal meeting venues and presentation rooms on all the floors, and a central library for shared use. Visual spark is overlaid on this framework of functional support, with wall graphics and furniture selections that play to themes such as 'sea and beach' and 'culture and youth', using distressed timber tables and wicker chairs, tables set on skate-board wheels and plastic school chairs.

Other facilities on the ground floor of the office block respond to additional aspects of the brief: an informal relaxation area for staff, a gym with machines and free weights room plus dance studio, treatment and steam rooms. A glass-fronted retail space runs the complete length of one wing facing 'the street'.

A model for sustainable living
The Pentland building meets its client's vision of a place where staff can enjoy working – and also play, relax, eat, shop, exercise and socialise – in a stimulating place. In addition to the facilities described, the campus incorporates a nursery for children aged three months to five years, two tennis courts and a five-a-side pitch. These amenities are commendable.

However, Pentland's content is not all. Its distinction is the design of a significant workplace building in a residential setting, with contextual sensitivity. The benefits this affords to employees and neighbours alike are considerable, showing the potential to develop worthwhile workplaces in suburban environments.

↗↗ Interior of office block, with workspace overlooking the building's main atrium, and bridges at varied intervals across the atrium length

↗ The point of it all: creating and sustaining a lively, creative workplace away from the central city core

ARCHITECTS
GHM Rock Townsend

CLIENT
The Pentland Group

PROJECT ADDRESS
The Pentland Centre Lakeside
Squires Lane
Finchley
London N3 2QL

AWARDS
British Council for Offices, 2003
 Best of the Best
British Council for Offices, 2003
 London Regional – Corporate
 Workplace Award
British Council for Offices, 2003
 National – Corporate Workplace
 Award
The Times / Gestetner Digital
 Office Collection, 2003
 Special Commendation

STRATFORD REGIONAL STATION

A railway station evoking optimism and confidence in its urban regeneration setting, by offering high standards of user comfort, security and safety, and creating a strong sense of place

The building meets a range of challenging requirements in a rigorous and inspiring way. Accommodating new rail tracks as well as different sets of existing lines, the project needed to resolve the complex interface between these different elements of infrastructure. The building's profile expresses its regeneration role with flourish, signalled by the signature curve of the roof and rear elevation. The dramatic glazed front elevation promotes the station's visibility from without and offers reassurance internally, with clear, well-lit space and open views to the platforms and the town, promoting confidence in its use.
The station's form and clarity contribute to its effectiveness as a positive new gateway in its urban context.

The brief

Stratford Station is a new surface-level building that incorporates an interchange between the London Underground's Jubilee Line Extension and existing rail lines. It serves as a terminus for the Jubilee Line and replaces a dilapidated station that served the North London overland rail service running north–south (parallel to the Jubilee Line) and the Central Line of the London Underground and Overland service running east–west. The brief was to create a single new transport interchange to serve the various train lines, and unify the identities of the various train services in a new transport interchange. The building also needed to be capable of expansion; it now also serves the extended Docklands Light Railway The site's significant banking to the northwest complicated the design challenge.

A second set of aims related to the regeneration of Stratford, for which the project was conceived as a catalyst. Specific objectives included a new civic hub with public landscaped square, a clock tower to celebrate Stratford's rail heritage, a new taxi rank, bus station and bicycle parking areas, road improvements and improved pedestrian links to the town centre and adjoining residential areas. The landscape around the station was designed by the architects and landscape architects.

The design was developed in close consultation with transportation bodies and local groups. Convenience and ease of movement were deemed to be critical to the project's success. Design of the building's layout, notably the location and size of the circulation routes, was informed by analysis of forecast passenger numbers. As the project was delivered in an operational setting, the existing tracks had to continue in operation through the construction period.

↖ Reassuring and uplifting: view across the upper walkway that traverses the train lines through the station, and overview of the concourse filled with light through the large glazed front elevation

Overview

The project comprises 4,000 sq m of new concourse accommodation on two levels, in an elegant rectangular building on a 100 m by 35 m footprint and 14 m high, constructed against the side of the embankment that accommodates the Central Line. The arrangement is determined by the position of the Overland rail line that runs through the station, dividing the concourse in two.

The building envelope evokes a strong external image. The roof sweeps upwards and forwards from behind the concrete upper-level walkway against the embankment, in a curve that projects over the 100 m long glazed front elevation. The front and side elevations are fully glazed, as is the lower part of the curved roof to the northwest.

The roof structure comprises a series of curved plate girder ribs. Each cantilevered girder is propped at its outer end on an inclined steel post that tapers in depth and width at both ends. These are linked by horizontal tubular members and diagonal bracing to form a huge Vierendeel truss along the whole south side of the building, carrying the glass. The loads are carried to ground level by four massive piers, positioned to avoid the rail tracks and the Channelsea River that runs under part of the site.

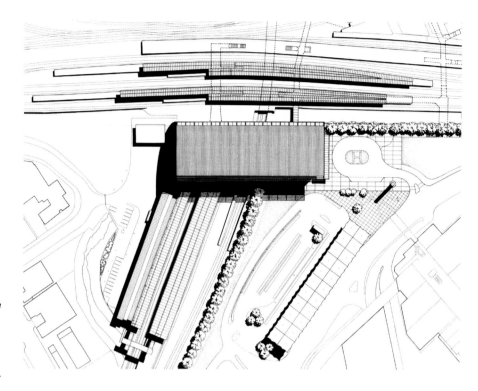

What Stratford Regional Station shows

Convenience and legibility

Stratford Station achieves the objective to provide a single space that integrates the various train lines it serves. The arrangement helps passengers to access the lines and change between them with ease. The building is entered at the eastern concourse where the main entrance faces Station Square, the bus station and taxi rank, with a fluent transition between outside and in.

The east concourse accommodates the ticket hall and retail space, with direct access to Platform 2 of the Overland line, and access by stairs, escalator or lift to an upper-level walkway, running along the northwestern edge of the building at approximately the same height as the embankment behind it. These routes are readily visible on entering the station. The upper walkway leads to and from the Jubilee Line platforms, and to Platform 1 of the Overland line, accessed via a separate staircase, escalator and lift on the western concourse.

Since 2007, the walkway also leads directly to the platforms serving the DLR. The platforms of the Central Line are reached from the lower concourse via two pedestrian tunnels – one new and one existing – as well as by lifts, with tunnel access also to the Overland platforms that are aligned with the Central Line. Although the Central Line platform is partly visible from the upper walkway, there is no access between the two, as space between the new building and the Central Line has been reserved for yet another line. Despite the complexity of the connections, the building succeeds as a unified space, providing clarity of direction and ease of movement for users. The staircase design facilitates comfortable circulation – with wide stairs, gentle gradients and substantial landings. The horizontal routes are also generous and well lit.

↗ Complex rail infrastructure accommodated by the station, with north-south lines running through it, and the parallel east-west lines running behind. The extended Docklands Light Railway now also forms part of this interchange

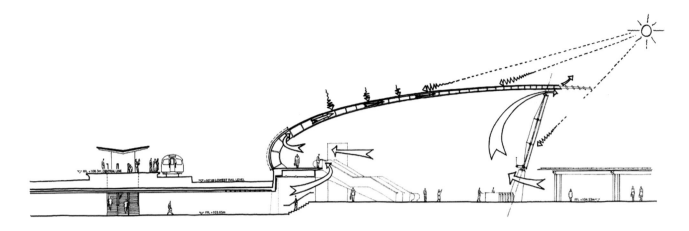

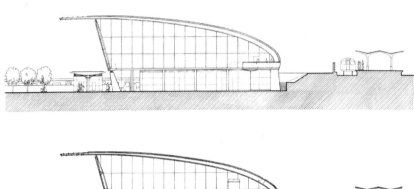

Safety and confidence

The regeneration objectives are well fulfilled with the station serving both as a beacon in Stratford, and a handsome and reassuring building to use. Its external appearance is striking. The curved roof – signalled in the contoured profile of the side elevations – and the large front elevation that inclines down and inwards, impart confidence through their sculptural conviction and visual transparency. This is reinforced by the visual connections between the interior and exterior.

The glazed front elevation faces both the bus station and the platforms of the Jubilee and parallel Overland lines, affording good views up to these platforms and making the station readily apparent to people approaching it from the south. This elevation also creates a welcoming presence by night. Floodlights on the gantry that runs along the bottom boom of the Vierendeel truss illuminate the silver ceiling.

Uplighters on the inner part of the curve add to this effect, whilst downlighters inside the station illuminate the shops and café at ground level. From the south, this horizontal band of light is prominently visible through the glazed elevation.

The expansive light and airy conditions inside the station are very comfortable, with the good sightlines and lighting promoting security and a perception of safety, both important factors in effective urban regeneration. Stainless steel balustrades on the upper walkway prevent objects being thrown or falling onto the track below.

↑↑ Diagram indicating the passive ventilation system, based on the roof void acting as a thermal flue drawing air across the concourse

↑ East elevation (above) and north-south cross-section showing the connecting subway (below)

The extensive glazing on the front and side elevations is key in creating the well-lit setting. This is enhanced by the roof design that also admits daylight through glazed cladding on the curved section behind the upper walkway. The palette of materials contributes further, with the extensive surface area encompassed by the light terrazzo floor playing an important part.

Sustainability with extensive glazing

The design provides for solar-assisted natural ventilation using the void in the double skin roof. Solar gain is limited by the projecting roof and sun louvers that shade the glass wall that faces southeast from high sun angles, and by the large overhanging eaves to the east and west. As the outer layer is heated, the 'stack effect' – causing warm air to rise and evacuate at the upper level – draws hot air through, maintaining air movement and comfortable summer temperatures.

Design for risk and durability

The structure addresses the need for resistance to collapse should a curved rib be destroyed or the front truss assembly be damaged, and the piers are designed to withstand the impact of flying metal. The stack effect also provides for smoke ventilation should a fire occur in the concourse. Self-finished materials and pre-fabricated elements were specified wherever possible, to promote quality control, ease of construction and longevity of performance in the building's life cycle.

The curved roof – signalled in the contoured profile of the side elevations – and the large front elevation that inclines down and inwards, impart confidence through their sculptural conviction and visual transparency.

↖   Inspiring confidence, regenerating a place: Stratford Regional Station's signature curve and luminous elevations by night and day

↗   Views inside out: the upper walkway with view to the parallel lines behind the building (top left); Stratford town centre and the bus station (top right); the concourse divided by the track – views in both directions (bottom right and left)

Technical achievement and user comfort
Stratford Station succeeds in
accommodating its complex infrastructure
whilst providing a high standard of
amenity for passengers as they access
trains and change between lines in
comfort. Its regeneration aims are
achieved by the confident stance it
assumes in its immediate urban context,
its optimistic profile and the reassuring
quality of its interior space with its strong
visual links to the exterior.

ARCHITECTS
Wilkinson Eyre

CLIENT
Stratford City Development
Partnership

PROJECT ADDRESS
Station Street
London E15 2HU

AWARDS
Aluminium Imagination Architectural
    Award for Extruded Aluminium, 1999
British Construction Industry Award,
    1999 – Commendation
Concrete Society Award, 1999
    – Commendation
Design Council, award of Millennium
    Product Status, 1999
RIBA Award, 1999
RIBA Civic and Community Award,
    1999
Shortlisted for the Stirling Prize, 1999
Structural Steelwork Award, 1999
    – Commendation
Civic Trust Award, 2000
Civic Trust Special Award for Urban
    Design, 2000
Structural Steel Design Award, 2000
    – Special Award

THE THIRD SPACE

A fitness and wellbeing club offering a wide range of specialist facilities, latticed together to form a coherent and exciting place in part of an existing building on a city-centre site

The Third Space demonstrates that a successful building can be achieved in awkward 'found' space, exploiting the excellent access opportunities of the city centre, creating value and generating a sense of surprise. The vision for the club was critical in recognising the property's potential. Skill and imagination were central in accommodating its uses with the necessary technical proficiency and providing for them with strong visual appeal. Key to the successful outcome is the mediation of daylight through a very small 'roof print' and down several levels. The designers' focus on providing visual permeability – vertically and horizontally – has resulted in volumetric variety, a welcome sense of expansiveness and intense visual engagement across the array of internal settings. The combination of original steel beams and strongly articulated contemporary insertions such as the staircases and dramatic flooring surfaces contribute to the building's frisson.

The brief

The client had found a seven-storey 1930s building in Soho close to Piccadilly Circus, in which the club occupies the basement, basement mezzanine, ground and first floors, with part situated below a courtyard. The objective was to accommodate a rich range of facilities within the volume available. The structure was gutted to free up the space. The facilities include three gyms – resistance, cardiovascular and freeweights – a 20 m swimming pool, a three-storey climbing wall, a hypoxic chamber offering a low-oxygen environment for high-altitude training, a competition-sized boxing ring, pilates studio, padded martial arts 'dojo', spa with pools, sauna and steam rooms and changing space for men and women. Facilities for wellbeing include a juice bar and a health centre offering general practitioner, sports medicine and complementary health services.

The brief for The Third Space was to create a club with a distinctive feel. This was focused on openness, with the aspiration for the interior to be filled with light and for members to enjoy a view of the sky. Visual connection was also sought between the various activities. The finishes were to be different from those in typical fitness environments.

As the space for the club was acquired on a 15-year lease purchased in 1999, there was strong pressure on the programme. The strategy was to appoint a lead architect to oversee the project and take responsibility for the layout and main circulation areas, allocating the interior design of the specialist uses to five different designers, with the lead architect involved in detailed briefings for function, spatial and environmental attributes, character and personality, cost and programme parameters. The client team visited other gyms as references from which to learn. The design of the medical facilities was informed by consulting practitioners. Some of the specific content evolved during the period of shell reconstruction and fit-out.

↖ Matrix of settings and visual links: martial arts dojo overlooking the swimming pool, itself covered by a glazed floor, admitting daylight to the pool and used as an activity area

Overview

The Third Space meets its challenging brief by accommodating most areas in sight of one another in a single large volume of space. Only the pilates and yoga studios, changing areas and medical suite are visually discrete. Where appropriate, glazed partitions afford acoustic segregation combined with visual permeability.

A total of 3,700 sq m is accommodated on four floors of different sizes, with two floors below ground level. The largest floor, of approximately 1,000 sq m, is on the bottom. It accommodates the swimming pool, changing facilities and a large studio for yoga and dance.

The floor above this – immediately below ground level – has a freeweights gym, with a competition-sized boxing ring and a martial arts dojo overlooking the pool. The entrance is at street level, through the 1930s elevation, to a dramatic, bright red reception desk and seating area in the lobby. Further seating is in a secluded linear space behind the Sherwood Street elevation. A café and juice bar in the lobby is run as an organic grocery store, directly accessible from inside the club, although the main entrance is round the corner on Brewer Street.

The other facility at ground level is the resistance gym, behind the lobby and above the freeweights gym.

Directly above this is the cardiovascular gym, with an enclosed pilates studio on the southwest corner, and the hypoxic chamber. This overlooks the lightwell that reaches from the glazed roof above the first floor to the lowest level, passing between the stacked gyms and the enclosed area of medical suites behind the Sherwood Street elevation. A second void extends from the upper-basement floor, through the two floors above, terminating under a glazed roof in the northeast corner and incorporating a climbing wall.

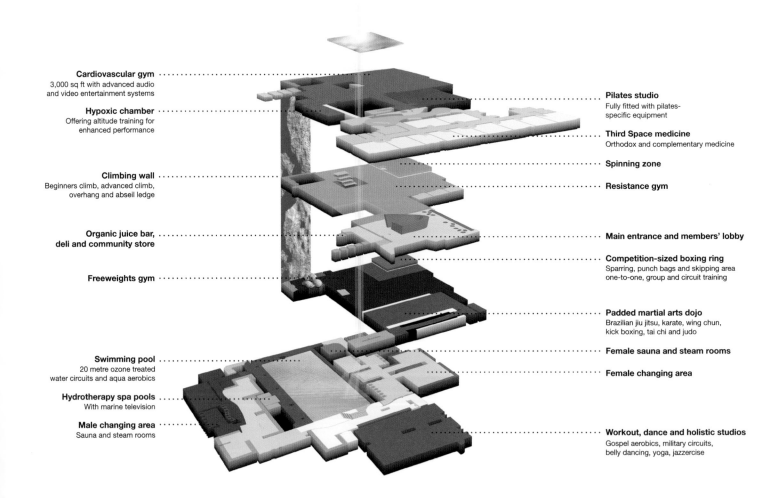

Cardiovascular gym
3,000 sq ft with advanced audio and video entertainment systems

Hypoxic chamber
Offering altitude training for enhanced performance

Climbing wall
Beginners climb, advanced climb, overhang and abseil ledge

Organic juice bar, deli and community store

Freeweights gym

Swimming pool
20 metre ozone treated water circuits and aqua aerobics

Hydrotherapy spa pools
With marine television

Male changing area
Sauna and steam rooms

Pilates studio
Fully fitted with pilates-specific equipment

Third Space medicine
Orthodox and complementary medicine

Spinning zone

Resistance gym

Main entrance and members' lobby

Competition-sized boxing ring
Sparring, punch bags and skipping area one-to-one, group and circuit training

Padded martial arts dojo
Brazilian jiu jitsu, karate, wing chun, kick boxing, tai chi and judo

Female sauna and steam rooms

Female changing area

Workout, dance and holistic studios
Gospel aerobics, military circuits, belly dancing, yoga, jazzercise

↑   Complex arrangement of spaces to optimise use of the available building volume, and promote participation by visual connections between the club's specialist areas

What The Third Space shows

Presenting opportunities

The complex matrix of spaces fulfils the brief's objective for excellent visual contact between the club's settings. The internal vistas at The Third Space are exciting, and the design is powerful in stimulating users' awareness of activities that they might not otherwise see. Contrasting materials reinforce the attraction of the respective areas: the bright red dojo, the glazed floor above the pool, the expanse of water. In combination, this palette is very exciting.

Natural light

The building's masterful vertical arrangement facilitates awareness of the sky even from two levels below ground. The lightwell enables daylight to pass through the two upper floors, and then through the glass floor at ground level. This centrally positioned glazed floor is dramatic both in itself, and for the views through it to swimmers in the pool below. Made of 40 mm toughened glass, it can be walked on, as well as used for activities such as stretch classes and a live disco. The feature is pivotal in expressing the club's ethos of inclusive participation. The dojo overlooks the pool, enabling visual contact between martial arts practitioners and swimmers, and also a view of the dojo from the poolside deck where club members lounge for relaxation. The pool is also seen from the central staircase. The glazed surface above it affords daylight and a sense of external awareness to swimmers.

Another powerful connecting feature is the climbing wall. This extends through three floors as a distinctive secondary lightwell. Natural light enters through its roof and passes down to all the activity areas.

The building's masterful vertical arrangement allows one to be aware of the sky even from two levels below ground. The lightwell enables daylight to pass through the two upper floors, and then through the glass floor at ground level.

↗↗ The achievement in bringing daylight into the club, with the climbing wall (to the rear of the image) extending upward to the small glazed roof area

↗ Reception area offering a view to the club and generating high impact on arrival through the retained 1930s façade

The design's visual openness promotes participation and natural light, and mitigates a sense of constraint from the building's restricted sectional heights and exposed steel columns.

Expansiveness and stimulus

The design's visual openness not only promotes participation and natural light, but also reduces the constraining impact of the building's restricted sectional heights and exposed steel columns. The materials enhance the sense of expansiveness – mirror-wall finishes, glass balustrading on the central staircase and glass fire doors framed in galvanised mild steel. These create a context in which the bright colours of the reception desk, boxing ring and dojo offer a sense of energy.

The design shows rigour and imagination in accommodating a demanding set of specialist uses in confined, unpromising conditions, bringing natural light and outside awareness deep into the building, and providing vertical and horizontal visual links that display and celebrate the club's activities, beckoning participation.

Promoting participation:
↑ Striking view to the swimming pool from the central stairs
↗↗ The glazed floor in full action
↗ Multi-purpose dojo: yoga in view of the pool

LEAD ARCHITECT/DESIGNER
Goldstein Ween Architects

DESIGN & BUILD ARCHITECTS
Collcutt + Hamp

CLIENT
Longshot Health and Fitness

PROJECT ADDRESS
13 Sherwood Street
London W1F 7BR

WELLCOME TRUST, GIBBS BUILDING

An extremely well-arranged and finely detailed office building that resolves the interface between its linear atrium, internal street and main working areas with distinction, and contributes to the pedestrian realm in its immediate urban setting

The Wellcome Trust's Gibbs Building shows successful engagement with the contrasting urban conditions on its busy Euston Road frontage and opposing quiet Bloomsbury elevation. A fine commissioned sculpture positioned close to the Gower Street elevation offers viewing interest to building users and passers-by. The atrium is unusually comfortable and uplifting – as a ground-floor street, as volumetric space, and in relation to both the adjacent office space as one rises up the building and the roof. The atrium elevations demonstrate a useful alternation of permeability and enclosure, and a refined use of materials and palette.

The brief

The Wellcome Trust, operating from its original building at 183 Euston Road and a number of disparate buildings in the vicinity, required a new headquarters on the adjacent western site to accommodate over 500 staff. The design needed to suit the institution's image as a leading scientific research fund. Other important Trust activities include consulting government on key matters of public policy, investment management, education, publishing, exhibitions, arts promotion, and developing its library and art collection.
The project brief was for a distinctive, timeless building appropriate to the Trust's international prestige, whilst avoiding flash extravagance.

As a workplace, the building needed to bring the administrative team together in an ergonomic and inspiring setting that fostered social interaction. As the owner-occupier, the Trust sought high standards of technical and qualitative performance, but also required the building to be approached as an economic commercial project.

Additional objectives derived from the building's context, with the intensely busy, traffic-ridden Euston Road and the relatively inactive hinterland of Gower Place at the northern edge of University College London's Bloomsbury estate. An appropriate relationship was needed with the Trust's original Greek Revival building that the new building would sit immediately beside to the west, and to which it would be linked internally up to third-floor level. Another particular requirement was the integration of Euston Square Underground Station within the scheme. The architects won the commission in a design competition.

← Upward view of Thomas Heatherwick's sculpture, Bleigiessen, at the atrium edge facing Gower Street

Overview

The Gibbs Building is on the south side of Euston Road. In addition to University College, numerous other major institutions are close by, including the new University College Hospital building directly opposite on Gower Street, and the British Library between Euston and Kings Cross.

The building comprises two parallel linear blocks, 90 m long, on an east–west axis. The 18 m deep, ten-storey high north block fronts Euston Road. A 9 m wide atrium separates this from the 9 m deep, six-storey high, parallel south block that is aligned with Gower Place. The arrangement provides almost 22,800 sq m of gross internal area, and just over 20,000 sq m net.

Constructed on a steel frame, the building is almost entirely clad in glass, based on a system comprising pre-fabricated triple-glazed façade cassettes.

The north elevation is modulated, with five towers separated by a recessed bay on either side of the central entrance and by two translucent stair cores. The recesses are formed by a 4.5 m stiff steel plate on each side, at 90° to Euston Road. These plates brace the building, provide the solidity for the fully glazed façades that enclose the recesses, and allow the interior space to be column free. The structure is expressed by exposed steelwork, bolts and cross-bracing. A series of 4.5 m deep double-height spaces – or 'mini-atria' – within the recessed bays is indicated externally by double-height cross-bracing. The services and ducts are concealed within the two stair cores.

The building can be entered from both Euston Road and Gower Place. The main entrance at the centre of the north elevation leads to a wide, double-height lobby and two large waiting areas that also serve as breakout spaces to the ground-floor meeting rooms on either side.

The base of the atrium, conceived as an internal 'street', is readily visible and reached directly from the lobby. The Gower Place entrance, on axis with the main entrance, is central in one's view on arrival. The internal street accommodates a café, informal seating and meeting areas, planting and a very large glass sculpture by Thomas Heatherwick, close to the Gower Street end.

The atrium rises to roof level above the ninth floor on the northern block, before sweeping down to enclose the top floor on the southern block. Above ground-floor level, the floor plates on the south block accommodate office space, with a restaurant on the fifth floor and an open suite for meetings or private dining at the western end. Floors one to eight on the northern block accommodate office space, with most of the ninth floor used for plant. The lift and WC cores, separate from one another, are in the northern block. Horizontal movement between the two blocks is via 4.5 m wide bridges across the atrium.

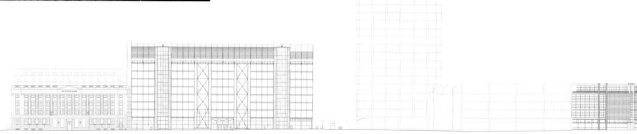

↑↑ The Gibbs Building, seen from the north-west, showing the taller elevation addressing Euston Road, and the curved roof over the lower block that is aligned with Gower Place

↗↗ Contextual response: short section, showing the building's setting to the north and south

↑ North elevation, showing the Gibbs Building's immediate adjacency to the Wellcome Trust's original Greek Revival building to the east, and the new University College Hospital building across Gower Street to the west

What Wellcome Trust Gibbs Building shows

Spatial quality

An effective but discrete glazed canopy signals one's arrival from the underground station beneath the building or along the busy Euston Road. On entering, the interior is immediately experienced as a highly legible and fluid sequence of spaces, at once serene and uplifting. The spacious double-volume reception lobby flows through to the internal street with the view of Gower Place beyond. The clear arrangement, spatial quality and sense of natural light are distinctive. The reception desk faces the front door. Behind the reception is the security office, elegantly housed in an open and transparent manner. The floor and reception desk are clad in French limestone, making the desk appear to float and contributing to the light and welcoming ambience in the space. Acoustically insulated glazed waiting areas on either side of the reception route expand the arrival area. Whilst contained and restful, these visitor areas provide a stimulating window onto the activity on Euston Road. This allows one to collect oneself and one's thoughts whilst still feeling in touch with the 'out there' that is the Wellcome Trust's concern.

Beyond this zone is the internal street, extending to the Gower Place elevation. This beautiful space is the heart of the building. Accommodating an array of informal settings and large Ficus Benjamina growing in limestone planters, it is also the route to the ground-floor conference seminar rooms, the office areas on the floors above, and the top floor restaurant with its southward roofscape views. The street is suffused with natural light that enters through the curved glass roof that encloses the restaurant atop the five-storey block. Natural light also penetrates through the fully glazed west and south elevations, and the east elevation above fifth-floor level.

The quality of light is extremely well modulated by fritting and perforated white fabric blinds on the glazed panels of the roof. The fritting provides a range of opacity, graduated up to 40 per cent. The blinds are controlled by the building management system.

Spatial modulation

The varied treatment on the atrium edges, as one looks up or down this volume, is rich in its mix of permeability and enclosure relative to the office areas behind it. The cores – on the atrium edge of the north block – are fully clad in maple, creating two solid panels up the elevation's full height. From the first to the fourth floors, all the office space is open to the atrium, although users can choose to draw down white fabric blinds at the open edge of the north block. Floors five to seven of the north block have a balustrade at the atrium edge, with sliding doors that people in the office areas can open or close. This variation reflects the change in thermal conditions as one rises up the building, given that the atrium is the return path for warm air. For this reason, the eighth floor is sealed with fixed panels.

The atrium proportions are extremely comfortable, and with the fluent connections to the adjacent spaces at both ground level and on above, it is simultaneously a distinct space and also the heart of the building that works and feels like a single place. The maple cladding that wraps the cores adds visual warmth and texture whilst providing acoustic absorption in the large atrium space.

Rich benefits from the artwork

The installation of Thomas Heatherwick's sculpture at the western end of the street is a masterstroke. Constructed on site, this specially commissioned work, Bleigiessen, comprises 150,000 glass spheres suspended by wire from the sixth floor. Its scale and position poise it to enrich the experience of building users – who see it in a dynamic way as they move around this part of the building – as well as attracting the interest of people outside the building, who can enjoy its shimmering luminance through the glazed elevation.

→   Westward view along the atrium base, showing the café, informal seating and meeting areas surrounded by ample circulation space, and benefiting from fine quality of light

Humane scale

Both the atrium and the office space have a more humane scale than a typical office building of this size, conveying a distinctive combination of airiness and intimacy. The scale of the linear office floor plates is reduced in several ways. The façade steps in and out on the north elevation and the floor plate steps back 4.5 m on the first floor of the north block and every alternate floor above it, creating the series of double-height atria. The linear feel is also modulated by the maple-clad lift and WC cores on the south edge of every floor in the north block. Equally proportioned, these core elements provide a rhythmic sequence along the floor plate. Another defining element is the 4.5 m opening in the central zone of the second floor and every alternate floor above it, enabling additional vertical connection via spiral accommodation stairs. Together these devices divide the 90 m run of space into a continuous series of smaller footprints. Essentially each floor has five suites of column-free office space, 12 m across by 18 m deep. All the spaces intercommunicate easily, benefiting from the clear horizontal routes, the supplementary vertical links and the generous bridges that link the north and south blocks.

Variety of experience

In addition to the varied experiences offered on the atrium base and with changes in users' view and position up the volume's height, the contrast between the atrium and the office floors offers further variety. The range is extended in the working areas themselves, with their sense of openness as well as containment, and their settings for individual work as well as collaboration between teams and work groups. The asymmetrical cross-section, mini-atria, connecting spiral stairs, and varying configurations of atrium screen afford a range of vistas and spatial experience. The variation encompasses a richness of settings, from the lofty conference rooms on the ground floor of the north block to the barrel-vaulted space at the attic level. The double-height mini-atria with their trees, positioned at intervals between the office suites, contribute further variety.

Sense of integration

In combination with its sense of spaciousness and the enriching floor plate variation relating to the perimeter atria and accommodation stairs, the Gibbs Building is lean.

Its structure of steel plates, expressed ties and concrete slabs is slender, and its integration of structural design and services is efficient. The use of materials – steel, glass and timber – is well balanced, offering simultaneous crispness and warmth. The metal is lightly coloured – grey, silver and white. The light-grey steelwork makes a tonal connection to the original Wellcome building next door. The extensive use of timber on the internal core towers and other areas of interior cladding work with the pale limestone flooring and planting to complement the steel and glass.

Environmental credentials

Despite being almost entirely clad in glass, the Gibbs Building's environmental design has achieved the Excellent BREEAM rating. The triple-glazed façade cassettes, incorporating a substantial cavity and silver louvered blinds, are designed to reduce solar gain and heat build-up during the summer and provide a pre-heated buffer to insulate the building during winter. In summer the cassettes also introduce ventilation, with fresh air brought in at floor level to the bottom of the outer layer, and hot air expelled through a vent at the top of the cavity. In winter, the process can be reversed. Heat generated in the offices rises and is cooled by chilled water in the ceilings, and hot air rises in the atrium, with heat reclaimed in the plant rooms on the top floor.

High reliance on daylighting – combined with glare reduction through the louvers, ceramic glass fritting on all the windows, solar control glass and blinds on the atrium roof – results in reduced use of artificial lighting. A comprehensive strategy for efficient lighting further reduces the energy load.

The quality of light is extremely well modulated by fritting and perforated white fabric blinds on the glazed panels of the roof.

← Effective use of the special spatial opportunity on the fifth floor of the south block: restaurant harnessing the excellent view, with blinds and fritting to modulate the light

Contextual response and public realm

The Gibbs Building shows a respectful stance towards its setting. Its scale and external appearance are well aligned with the original Wellcome headquarters next door. The two linear blocks are of different heights, with the ten-storey north block addressing the scale and activity of Euston Road, and the five-storey southern block recognising the more intimate nature of Gower Place. Large windows at pavement level on the Euston Road frontage provide display space for exhibitions, enriching the pedestrian route and adding to the significant artistic presence of the Heatherwick sculpture that faces Gower Street. Gower Place has become a one-way street from the east, and now incorporates a wider pavement with trees running alongside the Gibbs Building.

A civilising building, in and out

Overall, the Gibbs Building is distinguished by excellent organisation and an unusually high level of internal spatial quality. The proportions and detailing are finely judged and coordinated, achieving a fluent, facilitative and inspiring interior. The building makes a civilising contribution in its locality and gives apt expression to the ethos of the Wellcome Trust as its occupier.

Stimulating views in and out:
↑ Curiosity and wonder at the atrium sculpture (right), maintaining connection to 'out there' from the calm and quiet reception space (middle), interest for passers-by from the street level window display on Euston Road (right)
↗ View into the mini-atria facing Euston Road

ARCHITECTS
Hopkins Architects Ltd

CLIENT
The Wellcome Trust

PROJECT ADDRESS
Gibbs Building
215 Euston Road
London NW1 2BE

AWARDS
RIBA Award, 2005
Structural Steel Award, 2005
Art and Work Awards, 2006
    Outstanding Contribution to Art in
    the Working Environment
British Council for Offices Award,
    2006 – Corporate Workplace London
    Regional Award

WESSEX WATER

A light and airy office building with a connected series of interior spaces that flow down a banked site, affording all parts of the building with good natural light, fine views inside and out, and a pleasing human scale, and fostering a sense of community at a range of organisational scales

The building accommodates the office headquarters of a large utility company in a setting designated as an Area of Outstanding Natural Beauty. Wessex Water demonstrates responsiveness to this context by well-judged siting, massing and use of materials. Its design harnesses the site's character, both through its landscape treatment and by optimising the external views from within. The architecture provides a sequence of spaces, well proportioned to meet the needs of the staff as individuals and as a community. The project reflects an integrated strategy for sustainability, incorporating numerous measures to limit energy use. The interior is suffused with natural light, with the ambience simultaneously calm and stimulating.

The brief

Wessex Water's Operations Centre is an office building designed to accommodate some 580 people on a beautiful brownfield site (formerly housing an isolation hospital) in Claverton Down, Bath. The company's operations were formerly dispersed across separate sites, and the aims for the new headquarters were to consolidate these in one centre, promote operational efficiency and provide excellent working conditions for staff. A parallel aim was to facilitate openness, communication and collaboration, with space to encourage informality, stimulate teamwork and foster integration between departments.

Another key objective was sustainability, which Wessex Water perceived as important for their long-term business success. Their aspiration for a building that would be recognised as a positive model was linked to a framework for operations and services, encompassing a high-quality workplace, facilities that could be used by local people, 'stewardship' of landholdings and travel to work. The associated architectural brief included energy targets based on the building's whole life performance, with benchmarks for costs and energy use against which design decisions could be checked. In addition, the building had to reflect commercial criteria and present Wessex Water as a commercial business.

Overview

The resultant 10,625 sq m building is arranged in three parallel wings of two-storey office accommodation, linked by an internal street that provides the main circulation route and social spine. The site is sharply banked and the design response rakes the building profile across the gradient, with successive wings dropping down in a stepped sequence as one advances from the entrance block. The interplay between the internal and external settings is a strong feature in users' experience of the building.

Although the office wings are substantially clad in glass, providing a light and airy interior feel and promoting enjoyment of the landscape, the design integrates features for passive energy management to reduce the building's energy demands. The exposed pre-cast concrete coffered ceiling is an integral aspect of the servicing solution in the office areas, assisting in passive temperature control. The sculpted ceiling coffers are complemented by pre-cast concrete wall panels that also use thermal mass to store cool air, whilst adding visual interest to the glazed elevations.

The concrete ceiling rests on slender steel beams, with a single internal column dividing each office floor plate into two bays of 9 m and 6 m, with internal columns at 6 m centres along the wings. The 1.5 m by 1.5 m planning grid used in these wings coordinates with the 750 mm width of the coffered ceiling modules.

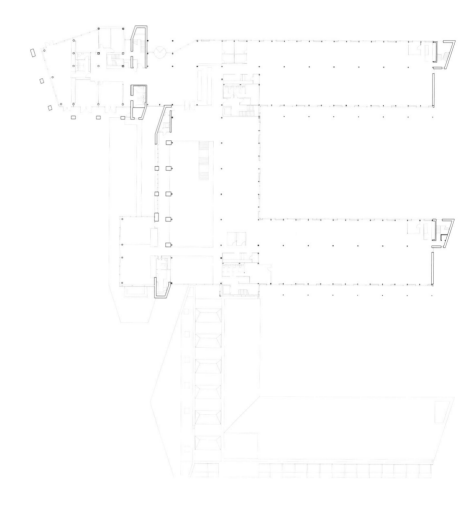

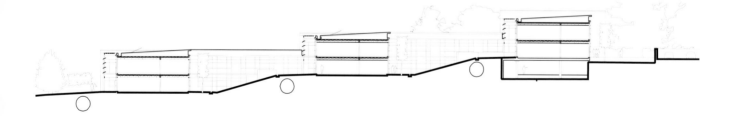

↑↑ 'E' plan: long arm accommodating the main circulation and social spine, and three office wings

↑ Section showing the raked building profile

→ Integration with the landscape: boundary enclosure – retained dry stone wall (left), Wessex Water's sensitive context (top right), the building stepping down across the gradient of the site

What Wessex Water shows

Responsive to the spirit of the site
The building shows the application of a well-integrated response to a sensitive, albeit brownfield, site. To the north, Wessex Water faces residential development. To the south, it borders an Area of Outstanding Natural Beauty overlooking the Limpley Stoke Valley, and has dramatic views over neighbouring woods to Salisbury Plain. Irregularly shaped, the site slopes sharply downward from the entrance, bounded by an existing dry stone wall that encloses mature trees.

The design harnesses this distinctive site character and minimises visual impact on the landscape. Existing trees and much local flora were retained, and meadow grasses were replanted as 'green roofs'. The selection of natural materials seen externally – glazed elevations, steel sunscreens on the south elevations and traditional Bath stone – intensifies the ethos of the locality.

Supportive spatial arrangement
The building is set back from the road, and its mass is reduced by a parallel sequence of low-rise blocks that step down across the site. The main building is E-shaped in plan, with each of the three 15 m wide prongs facing eastward to the open edge. These wings accommodate the open-plan workspace as well as office service areas, kitchenettes and WCs. The E's long arm accommodates the internal street, the open social settings – café and informal meeting area – close to the workspace. The double height and generous width of this space, and its openness to the adjacent workspace, contribute to the light and airy feel in the building interior, the visual connection between the respective spaces and the sense of spatial fluidity. The enclosed ancillary facilities – the restaurant and meeting rooms – are situated to the west of street.

The building cascades down the sloped site in three levels, with no part higher than two storeys. Two landscaped gardens that incorporate sculpture and water features sit in the two U-shaped external areas defined by the three wings. These enrich the amenity on the site, and reinforce the integration between the building's internal and external settings, affording fine views and the immediacy of the landscape presence inside the workspace.

Communication and ambience
The building's relaxed and comfortable interior feel derives from its extensive natural light, fine views, natural ventilation from openable rooflights and the airy ambience of its double-volume space. The design encourages the collaborative activity that was sought by the client.

The internal street is key in stimulating this. Its strong visual connection to the workspace serves as an icon that endorses communication and organisational integration. This is supported by its highly visible reference library, informal meeting space, café and the entrance to the restaurant. The street has a strong sense of place – as a route, as a central space, as a node and as the locus of the appealing settings it accommodates.

The arrangement and good internal sightlines make the range of settings easily legible, whilst modulating their scale and relationship to one another. The design succeeds in offering internal clarity and ease of access to the various settings. At the same time it articulates their distinctiveness. Unlike many contemporary office 'boxes', the interior at Wessex Water is not treated as a space differentiated only by its fit-out. The scale and arrangement of each wing and the settings on the street feel comfortable and complete both in themselves and in combination.

This is reinforced by the strong visual links between the respective interior spaces and their relationship to gardens between the wings. The scale of the zones is appropriate to the size of the smaller work communities that they accommodate, whilst the overall architecture provides a sense of inclusion in, and identification with, the wider organisation to which the individuals and departments belong.

Both the building's proportions and palette of materials play a positive role in shaping the users' experience, as does the awareness of natural light and external views wherever one is in the building. The interior feels at once gentle, comfortable and stimulating. This is reinforced by the quality of execution and consistent detailing of elements such as the joinery, the junctions of the steel beams and exposed concrete, the tooled Bath stone, and the metalwork on the windows and solar sunshades.

The green roof treatment is especially relevant on this stepped site where one regularly overlooks the section below. The pleasing building form and its appealing proportions and use of materials derive in large measure from its design for the sustainable agenda.

Passive air-handling

The arrangement facilitates natural cross-ventilation and passive cooling as the predominant mode of air-handling in the open plan. The position of the office wings on an east–west axis enables them to catch the natural wind. The office space is buffered from the afternoon sun by the enclosed spaces on the western edge of the street.

The orientation of the office wings, their design for natural ventilation, the building's thermal mass, and the siting of the ancillary accommodation to reduce solar gain, combine and work with other measures to reduce the building's energy use. These include the manually operated internal blinds and external sunscreens on the south elevation, and the use of solar panels to heat water. The building was designed to operate at less than half the energy consumption of a conventional office and the team report achieving CO_2 emissions of approximately 30kg CO_2 / sq m / year in the building's early phases of occupancy, significantly better than the prevailing best practice.

Integrated approach

The sustainable approach includes water treatment, with rainwater and surface water collected in large holding tanks beneath the landscaped areas, and the 'grey water' used to flush WCs and for irrigation. Porous paviours over a filter layer in the car park and paved areas allow surface water to percolate into the natural water table.

The pleasing building form and its appealing proportions and use of materials derive in large measure from its design for the sustainable agenda.

← The office space, comfortably scaled to the size of the work communities

↗ Flowing space, combining distinct expression of the different zones with strong visual links between them

The project strategy to promote lean design resulted in reduced embodied energy in the building's construction, by minimising the structure's requirements for steel and concrete, and specifying materials – like aluminium from hydro powered smelters – that involve low CO_2 emissions in their manufacture. The design incorporated useful innovations – such as the thin pre-cast vaulted slabs, placed between light steel beams, with a shallow concrete topping laid over the top to bind the whole construction together. The total structural floor weight is around half that of previous structures made entirely of concrete and achieves a similar visual and thermal effect, with a consequential reduction in foundation design.

Waste was further reduced by using recycled materials, such as crushed aggregate from concrete railway sleepers for the in situ concrete, and by selecting local materials to minimise emissions from transportation to the site, with the latter also promoting an indigenous feel.

Cut-and-fill calculations were employed to avoid needless removal of excavated material from site, with the associated waste and transport of waste that this involves.

An innovation in acoustics and lighting responded to the absence of finish on exposed concrete ceilings, with the adaptation of a standard pendant luminaire, providing indirect lighting to the ceiling coffers as well as direct lighting, to carry acoustic wings for sound absorption.

Wessex Water's sustainable design was recognised with an 'Excellent' BREEAM rating and 10/10 in the M4I's (Movement for Innovation) environmental performance index. The building has succeeded in meeting the client's requirements for environmental performance, institutional acceptability and an inspiring, effective workplace. It demonstrates the spatial and aesthetic quality that can be achieved with effective design for the green agenda that is of increasing importance to people both as citizens and as building users.

ARCHITECTS
Bennetts Associates

CLIENT
Wessex Water

PROJECT ADDRESS
Wessex Water Operations Centre
Claverton Down Road
Claverton Down
Bath BA2 7WW

AWARDS
Aluminium Imagination Award, 2001
British Construction Industry Award,
   2001 – Building of the Year
FX Award, 2001 – Large Office of the
   Year
RIBA Award, 2001
Steel Construction Institute, 2001
   – Commendation
RICS Award, 2002 – Building of the Year
RICS Award, 2002 – Low Energy Award

WEST RESERVOIR CENTRE, STOKE NEWINGTON

A new education and watersports centre incorporating a redundant water filtration plant on an urban reservoir, in a simple and elegant building that succeeds in its contemporary aims whilst respecting its legacy and context

The West Reservoir Centre effectively integrates old and new elements. The project harnesses a fine tower and water filtration plant as a dramatic central element, and adds two new empathetic wings, aptly scaled for the centre's young users. The design exemplifies a welcome sense of modesty and appropriateness for purpose, with its light-filled classrooms that face the water, and its external timber decking and pontoons. The approach demonstrates self-confident discretion in its scale, form and materials, facilitating one's appreciation of the heritage building and reservoir – both special in themselves – without unnecessary competition or distraction.

The brief
Developed for the London Borough of Hackney, the West Reservoir Centre is situated at a reservoir edge, off a main road in Stoke Newington. The project harnesses this valuable water amenity to create a purpose-built sailing centre in a highly accessible urban location, five minutes' walk from Manor House Underground Station, and entered from the local thoroughfare, Green Lanes. The building is designed around and incorporates a locally listed water filtration building that was no longer in active use.

When the reservoir was made redundant following the construction of the new London Ring Main, a local action group was established to seek community benefit from the site. Thames Water, the utility company controlling it, released both the West Reservoir and the New River to the London Borough of Hackney for recreational and educational purposes. This would enable local children to receive water sports instruction close to where they live, avoiding the need to travel to the next nearest facility in the Lee Valley.

The brief to convert the legacy building to a watersports and environmental centre was formulated with active assistance from staff experienced in running relevant training courses. The aim was for a simple building to celebrate the plant's original purpose, with new facilities to serve the centre's contemporary functions. Following their appointment, the architects worked with the future centre's proposed managers to develop the detailed brief. The scheme design was presented to the public and Hackney Councillors, and the local community was consulted at every stage. Following discussion between the client, future management team, borough education officer, school children and the design team, the decisions were made to retain the original tower and replace its wings with new enlarged accommodation. The architects joined Hackney Arts to select and involve an artist to collaborate on the project.

↖ Successful integration: respectful of its legacy assets, effective for its current function, a gentle vista for residents in the neighbouring housing

Overview

The building's centrepiece is the retained tower that has been opened up internally. It accommodates the entrance, reception area and exhibition space. In place of the two previous low wings on either side of the tower are new single-storey glass and steel portal framed structures that accommodate the classrooms, changing rooms, offices and associated ancillary space.

The tower's footprint is 11 m by 24 m and its structure four storeys high. The design has revealed both the tower's internal steel frame and the equipment associated with the former filtration use – the wash water storage, air compression tanks and pipework. These elements are now visible and offer interest up the tower's height. The windows are prominent, with a direct view of the water through the lower band of windows on the tower elevation facing the reservoir, whilst the upper band suffuses the interior tower with natural light.

The new wings, both 32 m long, are arranged symmetrically on either side of the tower. Their structure comprises clear span steel portals at 5.4 m centres, extending beyond the building envelope and expressing their function on the exterior. Most of the centre's indoor functions are accommodated in these wings. A circulation route runs down each wing, on the central axis from the entrance hall at the base of the tower. The space between this route and the north-facing elevation addresses the reservoir, with the teaching and meeting spaces situated in this 6 m deep zone. The ancillary facilities are accommodated in the 6 m zone between the circulation spine and the south elevation that faces the car park. The south and side elevations are clad mostly in terracotta tile. The north elevation facing the water is fully glazed with low emission double glass to reduce solar gain.

The remaining elevations are relatively solid and clad in terracotta tile, with the only openings being a glazed door to the central route that provides an entrance on each side of the building, and a narrow band of high-level glazing across the south elevation.

The external timber structures are another key set of elements. A new hardwood deck with boardwalk, floating pontoons and jetties extends from the building to the water's edge. The canoe store is in a separate timber structure, with semi-open vertically slatted sides.

Removing its first floor slab has created a dramatic space and afforded an experience of the tower's expansive volume that has particular value in the urban context.

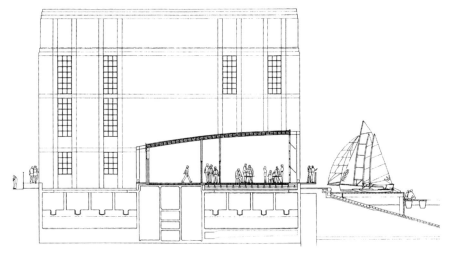

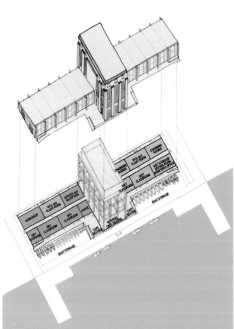

← Cross-section of new wing against water tower

↑ Simple arrangement of circulation and accomodation in the new wings

↗ Sympathetic integration of old and new elements

↗↗ The tower as a space with special attributes: heritage, volume, aspect and light

What the West Reservoir Centre shows

A breathing space in the urban fabric

The building is exemplary in all its principal capacities – as heir to the filtration plant, custodian of the water amenity, facilitator to the children who use it as a learning base, and neighbour to the surrounding buildings.

Retaining the tower was key to the building that now exists. Removing its first floor slab has created a dramatic space and afforded an experience of the tower's expansive volume that has particular value in the urban context. The views from the tower to the reservoir's expanse of water, ringed by the housing blocks beyond, reinforce the centre's distinctive attribute as an uncluttered oasis.

Expressing the building's heritage value

The building's heritage is promoted by the tower's revealed steel frame construction. Both the frame and the retained filtration equipment have a strong sculptural impact. This is set off by the volume inside the tower, and reinforced by blue lighting effects. The lighting design by the artist Charlie Holmes focuses on the tower interior, highlighting the compression tanks and the underside of the water tank. Two decorative cast plates are set into the floor – one at the entrance, the other at the base of the tower. These features, attractive in themselves, enrich the centre's historic and current sense of place by describing attributes of water. The spatial quality, surface treatments, sculptural reliefs and lighting work together to celebrate and promote an appreciation of the building's distinctive legacy.

Inspiring and effective functional space

For its immediate 'here and now' purpose of instruction, the building provides light and airy classroom accommodation with fine views of the water. To fulfil these objectives, the building depends on its new wings. These are sympathetic to the retained tower, whilst being entirely contemporary in design. Externally, the old and new elements form a well-integrated composition. The wings' roofline echoes the light horizontal bands on the tower's elevations. Their exposed external structure resonates with the tower's tall windows and the terracotta cladding harmonises with the brick tower.

Appropriate and sustainable

The space in the new wings is clearly arranged and pleasant to use, with efficient, easy routing, good views of the water from the classrooms and meeting spaces, and reliance on natural daylight without undue solar gain. With the high ceilings that enable the space to be naturally ventilated, the design promotes energy efficiency and low running costs, furthered by the 200 mm insulation on the underside of the roof. Whilst the classrooms are heated by perimeter radiators, the tower has electric heating within the new floor slab, providing heat at the level at which people use the space and avoiding heating the entire large volume.

Interface with the setting

The boardwalk and floating pontoons play a key role in the centre's objectives to teach watersports and promote their enjoyment. These timber structures provide access for active use of the water, as well as valuable space where participants can rest, have lunch and enjoy the views at the water's edge. Seen from the reservoir, these surfaces form part of the engaging visual matrix that constitutes and defines the centre.

Boats are stored on covered filter beds by the edge of the reservoir. The canoe shed is constructed in a darker timber that blends modestly into the backdrop of the brick housing block situated between the centre and Green Lanes.

The building is exemplary as heir to the filtration plant, custodian of the water amenity, facilitator to the children who use it as a learning base, and neighbour to the surrounding buildings.

The building's contemporary function as an urban centre to promote education and watersports:
↖ View from the jetty
← Taking a break on the deck, facing the water, with the glass-fronted classrooms behind

↗ The neighbours' view by night: artistic lighting solution harnessing the reservoir for reflection

Triumph of modesty

The West Reservoir Centre offers
spatial quality, clarity and convenience,
with simple elegance and a fitness for
purpose. It demonstrates the benefits
that can flow from celebrating heritage
elements and integrating old and new with
functional and aesthetic effectiveness,
and without recourse to pastiche.

People from the local community worked
with Hackney Borough Council to identify
the opportunity for this centre. The
outcome as built endorses their vision.

It has benefited from the early dialogue
with the sailing instructors to inform
the brief and the architects' well-judged
responsiveness in meeting the aims
without 'over-egging the cake'. They
have created a successful place that is
about watersports, water as a resource,
education, legacy, enjoyment and amenity
in the city.

ARCHITECTS
Marks Barfield Architects

CLIENT
London Borough of Hackney

PROJECT ADDRESS
Stoke Newington West Reservoir
Centre
Green Lanes
London N4 2MA

AWARDS
Civic Trust Award, 2002

BUILDINGS THAT FEEL GOOD: LESSONS FOR DESIGN

What can buildings offer over and above shelter and safety? And what of the cost? With the contemporary rate of construction, much of it replacing existing building stock, these questions have an urgent bearing. The immediacy is also linked to the forceful rise of 'value engineering', often a euphemism for cost reduction. How could this succeed by reference to price alone, and if the inherent values in buildings' capacities to affect people are neither recognised nor appreciated? What of the firmness, commodity and delight of Vitruvius?

Firmness and commodity are certainly here. There are basic levels at which user requirements are now acknowledged (if not fully understood), with a widespread acceptance that they must be addressed.

At the level of individual buildings, there is clear recognition of safety and ergonomics, often involving a fine line between them. Once they are defined as safety issues, building and fire regulations underpin their attention. Beyond this, ergonomic considerations have become allied to the 'productivity agenda', based on a connection that is now discerned between internal environmental comfort and human performance. Effective comfort conditions (and scope for users to influence, if not control, them) are associated with a higher standard of activity inside.

Productivity measures are defined as increased commercial turnover, improved educational attainment, shorter patient recovery periods and so on. In the earnest desire to prove the connection between productivity and design, the odd statistic is vaunted (not always in context). Meanwhile the search to find this 'holy grail' through 'key performance indicators' hovers around the research agenda, despite generating fewer substantive results than hoped for.

The growing environmental agenda has added impetus to the focus on design to achieve interior environmental comfort. The aim to provide for user comfort with zero, or at least reduced carbon impact, prompts the relevance of understanding users' tolerance to, and satisfaction with, the outcome conditions that alternative design approaches can deliver.

A related focus is at the level of organisations. Formerly, organisational interest centred on efficient use of space, and, given the cost of procuring and occupying buildings, this continues to be a strong objective. Its recent overlay – that wasteful space usage is not only uneconomic financially but also profligate environmentally – adds social legitimacy to the commercial drive for efficiency.

The interest in space efficiency has been followed by the recognition that space should also be effective. These efficiency and effectiveness agendas, both integral to building design, can pose mutual conflicts. An example is the optimum approach to the design of staircases. In an office building, narrower, more compressed stairs facilitate core efficiency, allowing for a greater proportion of rentable space, whilst wider, shallower stairs, designed for elective rather than emergency use, are more effective in their likeliness to promote casual social interaction – now a common organisational objective. The dissolution of the ring fence around efficiency objectives heralds competition between parallel aims that cannot be resolved without a vision for the building's use, and hence a vision for the building. Even with a 'decision-making process' to weight and prioritise the respective objectives involved, and even where such processes remain implicit, a vision is needed to determine priorities.

The interplay between efficiency and effectiveness is also apparent in any building's capacities to accommodate internal planning – its facilitation or frustration of alternative layouts. The layout is central in determining how individuals will experience a given space, but the layout's conception is typically at the level of the organisation, driven by the need to 'fit the organisation into the space'. In this process, the discourse (such as it is) centres on 'headcount', rather than on individuals' experience of how a building and its spaces 'feel'. This accounts for the specialism of 'change management' that has come into recent play. Whilst this could entail shaping a building to its users, *that* process is called design, whereas change management is commonly seen as adjusting users to the building.

What then of individuals' perceptions and sensibilities? – back to Vitruvius and the substance of delight. It takes a commitment in mindset as well as a shift of language to put oneself in users' shoes. And it takes authority and leadership to command a voice for future users' experience on project teams and in design meetings.

Apart from available skill and knowledge, numerous other challenges surround the introduction and advocacy of user experience in design development. One impediment is the nature of user data, with its inherent degree of 'softness' relative to engineering metrics, even when researched user responses are systematised, rated, aggregated and compared. Impatience is another barrier, with the frequent insistence on having brief answers – preferably those one wants – on tap.

Perhaps the most important barrier is building complexity, the multiplicity and interaction of the elements that define built spaces (independently of the numerous social factors that also define users' experience). What correlations, in any study, is one able to make between users' reactions and the specification of this or that? The results are never simple. Rather, the learning acquired from successive studies with building users is iterative and incremental. Developing an educated understanding of the influence of certain design features, and the difference that an alternative approach may make, is a journey. One learns from experience. Its acquisition takes time.

Hence the origin and purpose of the lessons to be distilled from the case studies in this book. They serve as shortcuts to provide insight in support of the quest to learn how buildings can be designed to feel good. Individually and collectively, these buildings' clients and designers have formulated articulate and stretching visions, and succeeded in their effective design expression and translation.

Twenty exemplars, each with a lesson? That was the plan. Despite the criterion that if a case study demonstrates good practice on even one aspect that is not typically well addressed, that would be sufficient, all the exemplars demonstrate a wider range of instructive themes. Their recurrence strengthens the recognition of these aspects' relevance in enriching people's experience of buildings, as both inhabitants and passers-by.

Lesson 1

Beyond the building: creating external value

Several of the case studies highlight the significant contribution that can be made where a design project encompasses more than the building limits, and an effective vision for such wider reach is developed. Chiswick Park is most persuasive in demonstrating this point, with its visionary masterplan that conserved the central area of the campus as a pedestrian zone, at a critical mass that enables its generous approach to hard and soft landscaping to create a new amenity space of distinctive scale and quality. Post-occupancy research with people working at Chiswick Park shows immense user appreciation of this asset. The necessary strategic decision to prevent vehicle access to this zone nevertheless represented a commercial risk that the quality of design implementation has helped to mitigate. Another departure was designing the park for access by users who are not members of the tenant organisations. This makes the campus and its facilities valuable local assets. It also affords a sense of connection to the wider realm that is welcomed by people who are based on the park.

The creative potential to be a force for good beyond the building itself is further illustrated by other exemplars. Pentland's wonderful bridge over the lake, its rich palette that echoes the building exterior, and the project's investment in restoring the lake to a conservation standard, have resulted in a luscious setting. At the Stoke Newington West Reservoir Centre, the timber decking outside the building, with its boardwalks and pontoons, greatly extends the user amenity offered by the building.

The Mailbox shows that the potential to add to a setting is not constrained by land ownership nor limited to the visual impact of a building's form. The development has been well integrated in the Birmingham townscape. The project encompassed a lighting scheme above the pedestrian passage below the elevated road that runs past the building, and a fine ramp for people to negotiate the change in levels between the outdoor cafés and the public towpath beside the canal at the rear of the building. Both these features make walking to and through The Mailbox a fluent aspect of pedestrian enjoyment in Birmingham.

The Wellcome Trust's Gibbs Building makes the point that design can contribute to the public realm without physically extending into it. Its exhibition windows along Euston Road and the placement of the large Thomas Heatherwick sculpture close to its Gower Street elevation both contribute to users' experience in the public realm.

Lesson 2

Beyond the building: response to context

The next layer of spatial influence is the building's impact on its context. The approach to the Mersey Valley Processing Centre highlights the fundamental work that can be done to achieve positive results. The analysis and re-thinking of the processes undertaken within the centre led to a strategic uncoupling and regrouping of processing activities, enabling their encapsulation in a number of buildings articulated around the precise functions that each accommodates.

The Ercol case study also illustrates wider contextual benefits from re-thinking industrial processes. In this case, the achievement has been to reduce the factory's previous levels of acoustic impact, and hence its intrusion on residents who live near the site. Reviewing the factory's traditional processes achieved the important internal benefit of identifying a non-flammable furniture spray, a critical step in facilitating the factory interior being designed as a single large spatial volume.

The office exemplars illustrate responsive approaches to urban conditions as well as localities of lower density. The positioning of Wessex Water on its site sets the building back from the neighbouring residential buildings, and its raked profile across the sloping site limits its mass at all points in this sensitive area of outstanding beauty. The Gibbs Building, in its dense urban setting, addresses the tough conditions of the busy Euston Road with a ten-storey height, dropping to five storeys on the quieter Gower Place elevation and according with the lower prevailing height in northern Bloomsbury.

The contrast in conditions facing the back and front of The Mailbox is more striking still. The building meets this challenge admirably, with the bold 32 m high elevation addressing the elevated ring road that passes by its front elevation, the terraced design that steps down gently to the intimate canalside at the building's rear, and an effective mediation in the scale of the building's main sections as it achieves the necessary transition between these contextual responses.

Lesson 3
Form and place-making
Several of the exemplars demonstrate the use of building form to help define or lift their context. The signature profile of Stratford Regional Station accents the building and promotes the social confidence that is important to local regeneration. The City of Manchester Stadium signposts East Manchester, providing a strong visual marker from afar, and an exhilarating sculptural presence at near distance as well as inside the building. With its combination of vertical and horizontal elements, the stadium's form works as a magnet for its locality at every range from which the building is seen and experienced.

At the other end of the scale is the Café on the Square at Brindleyplace. In some sense, the café's form *is* the building. Without this, it would be any kiosk or coffee stand. In the event, this minnow of a building exudes the power to signify the whole main square of Brindleyplace. Its curvaceous form against the backdrop of the orthogonal office buildings that surround it is like a life force. The Oxo Tower Restaurant contributes to the new sense of place that the development has brought to this quarter of Southwark, as a high-level frieze of activity on the terrace by day, and a radiant band of illumination by night.

North Greenwich Underground Station has mastered the challenge of creating a sense of place entirely below ground, modelling the building to help define this. The subtle maritime echoes in the station's form act as a trigger in visualising the station's external context and reinforce one's sense of connection to the locality that remains invisible whilst one is inside the building. Abbey Mills Pumping Station draws on its striking and memorable form to develop the sense of place on its legacy site, give the building contemporary expression and maintain its image in the mind long after it has been seen.

Lesson 4
Social memory with contemporary functionality
The physical expression of tradition can be overt or subtle. It is not the re-use of a legacy building per se that offers this – the association needs to be comprehended or felt. Several of the case studies nourish a sense of social memory, and achieve this whilst providing for contemporary functionality and without resort to pastiche. The two most obvious examples are the Oxo Tower building and the West Reservoir Centre, both symmetrically arranged around a legacy tower to which the current functions that the architects have assigned them is to tell the buildings' stories. The adapted warehouse building that is now the mixed-use Oxo Tower has a generic reference to its former use. The tower, with its illuminated red OXO lantern, makes this link specific. So too for the watersports centre, with the historic pumping equipment now displayed as a vertical arrangement of interpretive sculpture inside the former water tower, and the former functional association again made specific in the cast bronze reliefs set in prominent positions in the floor. The remodelling of both buildings is without compromise to their current functions – housing, studios and dining at Oxo Tower; education in watersports and the environment at the West Reservoir Centre. The approach that underpins these adaptive interventions shows confidence in the contemporary solutions, alongside a recognition of the value that resides in the buildings' heritage elements.

A similar approach can be seen with The Third Space, where the original façade is intact, and the strikingly modern interior is structured around the original exposed steel columns. The layers of building history are like a palimpsest, in this case revealing a sense of the building's former life rather than its former use, with the interplay of old structure and new environment generating a stimulating frisson.

The expression of social memory differs again at Abbey Mills and at RADA. The pumping station's lineage is evident in its fine brick neighbours. The new building's acknowledgement of its succession in this line is through the evocation of symbolism and its translation to contemporary form. At the Jerwood Vanbrugh Theatre, the strategy focused on selective demolition and retention, with the new building entirely contemporary both in function and design expression, and the smaller old building (in its now substantially adapted form) as a custodian of the academy's inspiring 'ghosts' and illustrious alumni.

Lesson 5
Interface between the interior and exterior

Lessons 1 to 4 centre on how a building can relate *to* and what it can do *for* its setting. The focus shifts here to what its setting can do for the building.

A setting that encompasses a variety of conditions, as at The Mailbox, offers obvious scope to define a development with variety in scale and ambience. The Mailbox design has harnessed this opportunity, with the most obvious benefit being its range in functions and moods, generating synergies in the building's scope to meet different user needs. Two significant respects in which the building borrows from its external setting are the modulation at the rear to optimise waterside views for the bars and restaurants, and the decision to open the long shopping street to the sky. Whilst some shoppers may prefer an enclosing canopy overhead, a design that resists 'interiorisation' offers a distinctive experience in a less hermetic realm.

Height offers the inherent prospect of panorama. The majestic waterside view from the Oxo Tower Restaurant is so remarkable that it risks eclipsing the fact that other views from high locations are also valued. The point is underscored by the richness of the southward views that the restaurant design facilitates. At Citigroup, the roaming views to the north and south from every floor through the atrium's external elevations afford the exploration of extensive tracts of London. The level of elevation does not have to be particularly high in absolute terms to offer an enriching experience: the Gibbs Building's southward view of the Bloomsbury roofscape is from the fifth floor.

A particular lesson from the Oxo Tower is the social value of a public viewing gallery, coupled with the knowledge that such provision – in this case stipulated by the landlord – is feasible in association with a commercial restaurant operation and residential units below. The design of the Oxo Tower Restaurant is also instructive in its approach to the large glazed front elevation that evokes a wonderful sense of 'being in the sky', and the care taken to avoid night-time reflections in the glazing so as not to spoil patrons' northward views across the river. The Citigroup building offers a high-level terrace, a feature that users value, particularly given the changes in work style and technology that now facilitate informal modes of working outdoors.

Wessex Water, Ercol, Pentland and Chiswick Park – in different ways – exemplify how design can capitalise on the external landscape, incorporating it into users' experience inside a building. The entire arrangement of Wessex Water and its disposition on the site optimise occupants' connection to the outside from the building interior. The design of the three wings gives extensive visual access to the courtyard gardens that they enclose. The wings' stepped arrangement enhances the connection to the outdoor landscape by enabling views from the higher wings to the green roofs below.

At Ercol, the strategy to capture the landscape view right across the factory's large elevations is distinctive, particularly as the effort that is made to nurture factory workers is not usually on a par with the attention paid to attracting and retaining 'knowledge workers' in white collar employment. As the vistas at Ercol are woodland views, and the factory is centred on furniture manufacture, the direct engagement with the building's setting has special relevance in giving workers an experiential association with the life cycle of the products that they make.

At Pentland, the rich interplay between the interior and exterior centres on the building's social areas. The timber decking that wraps around the glazed elevations of the foyer and restaurant blocks overlooking the lake, extends the building into the landscape and brings the landscape into the building. A similar role is performed by the timber boardwalk and pontoons at the West Reservoir Centre, with the decking extending the building to the water, functionally as well as visually. The visual connection to the architecture and landscaping from the building interiors at Chiswick Park is promoted by the greater than typical floor-to-ceiling height and the full perimeter glazing, enabling an appreciation of the fine external setting even from deep on the floor plate.

Harnessing the exterior is not just about panorama and landscape. The Issey Miyake store and the Gibbs Building both exemplify the point that a window on city life can endorse a building's rationale and add meaning to users' experience. The dissolution of the barrier between out and in at Issey Miyake not only serves to 'invite participation', but the taxis, cars and pedestrians that pass by reinforce the recognition that the context of fashion is social rather than private. Awareness of the bustling Euston Road from the elegant and serene waiting areas in the Gibbs Building's reception area serves to connect the well-endowed Wellcome Trust with the sense of social purpose underlying its activities.

The small interior space at the Café on the Square at Brindleyplace would indeed feel confined without the clear visual connection to the surrounding square, onto which the building also opens up and into which it spills in fine weather. For the Mersey Valley Processing Centre, the scope to see into the centre is critical in reducing its mystique and forging acceptance of its function in this location. For those inside the building, the views out are a welcome connection to the 'outside world' from an operational setting that is manned by just a small number of people.

Lesson 6

Natural light, sun and shadow

Of course, 'the outside' is more than views to landscape, panorama and urban life – privileged or gritty. Outside equals daylight, and building users LOVE this resource. All my occupancy studies highlight 'light and airy' as high on the range of factors that promote satisfaction inside buildings. In the way that users express this, it is first and foremost about delight. The scope for natural light to reduce dependence on artificial light comes across as secondary, though recent studies where the balance of artificial light has not been considered favourable show people to be dissatisfied, in part by the quality of artificial light, but also because they resist its energy demands where these are perceived to be unnecessary.

The exemplars underscore the fundamental way in which natural light can create a high-quality interior experience. The refinement and clarity that this lends at Wessex Water and in the Gibbs Building are very uplifting. At Issey Miyake and EMI, the pleasure of the light is complemented by the play of shadow, with the added richness of effect at Issey Miyake from the multitude of mobile petals suspended from the lighting feature, casting dynamic shadows on the walls. The Ercol production staff enjoy conditions suffused with natural light through the glazed elevations and the polycarbonate toplight that runs the full length of the factory. Passengers at Stratford Regional Station benefit from station conditions that sparkle. Children at the West Reservoir Centre learn in classrooms suffused with daylight and addressing the water. Spectators at the Manchester City Stadium sit in stands that are day-lit from the back as well as in front – all the way round the building.

The enormous difference that daylight makes is underscored in the complex matrix of spaces at The Third Space, with light brought down the building's multiple layers and through the confined roof area, including the climbing wall that rises to its glazed cover above. The commitment to achieving this is well rewarded. A similar vision is apparent in the design of the cleft in the Jerwood Vanbrugh Theatre, where – as in The Third Space – daylight is brought to basement level through a glazed floor.

With all their celebration of natural light, the irony is that users often suffer from too much. The exemplars are fulsome in demonstrating the need to manage lighting impacts and solar gain in buildings with large areas of glazing. Most strategies use a combination of measures. The mix of elegant fritting and blinds on the glazed roof panels at the Gibbs Building, and the atrium-facing blinds that individual users can control, are added to the now well-established use of louvers, to give the occupants a particularly well-modulated quality of light with a level of direct individual control.

Pentland shows two contrasting approaches, with the overhanging eaves and external louvers that manage the impacts in the building's common spaces, and smaller windows with a high ratio of opacity in the brick elevations of the office block. At Nexus, call-centre workers' preference for lower levels of light as a context for their intensive screen-based work is addressed by the active management of daylight through all five elevations, including the narrow window band along the sides and rear, and the ten large round EFTE foil-covered apertures that modulate daylight entering through the roof.

Lesson 7
Sustainability has many aims

The sustainability agenda has been focused on carbon reduction and the depletion of non-renewable resources, seeking to limit buildings' energy in use and specifying materials from renewable sources. The factors that impinge on this are extensive. With the energy consumed in reaching a building an important part of the overall equation, location and access are key. The energy embodied in an existing structure is also relevant in evaluating alternative development strategies that may pose adaptive re-use against demolition.

The utility that a building can provide is another central aspect. More intensive usage, and the flexibility to accommodate alternative uses should the initial function cease to be relevant, both offer potential scope to avoid the construction of buildings that may not be necessary, with all the associated savings in environmental impact – in the land and materials that these buildings would consume, in travel between them and in their servicing. Chiswick Park exemplifies particularly efficient use of a site, providing a high ratio of accommodation on the site area, whilst simultaneously, its excellent masterplan affords a valuable sense of spaciousness and amenity to users.

The design strategy for Nexus, to accommodate the call centre required by the client, with the scope to convert the building for an industrial use such as production or warehousing, illustrates another aspect of sustainable practice. Such an approach may also make associated sense as a financial investment, although from both the financial and environmental perspectives, caution is warranted against over-specification, as features relating to potential alternative uses can easily prove to be superfluous and redundant. Nexus demonstrates the more sustainable route – to arrange the building shell to afford flexibility, with scope for later adaptation of services if required. The productive strategy for the City of Manchester Stadium to accommodate two successive major events, and its design to sustain a high level of use in the building's second phase, offer a powerful and timely exemplar of an approach that avoids 'white elephants' – another essential aim of sustainable development.

The Mailbox, EMI, The Third Space, the Oxo Tower building and the West Reservoir Centre all illustrate the successful re-use of existing structures. In each case, their respective design visions were pivotal in creating the renewed value released by their current use. The social dimension of sustainability is central in designing buildings that feel good. The Oxo Tower building and the West Reservoir Centre both contribute by incorporating valuable expressions of social memory, enriching people's recognition of the past whilst supporting contemporary needs.

The Pentland building is significant as a high-quality appealing workplace that invokes design to challenge the assumption that creative industries can only recruit the right staff in city centres. Its successful design vision and implementation offer a model for creating other fine workplace buildings in suburban areas, promoting scope for people to negotiate their work and family involvements with less personal wear and tear – a basic platform for social sustainability. And Ercol's provision of fine workplace conditions for all its workers exemplifies another important social strand. Buildings can contribute to uplifting people's experience in their workplace; factories need not be exceptions. What are needed are clients with social visions and an instinct for the role of design in fulfilling them, and designers with the imagination and skill for their realisation. The role of Stratford Regional Station in fostering confidence, both in the building's use and in the locality as a place, shows the powerful role of design that makes people feel good in promoting regeneration and social sustainability.

These points illustrate the scope for wide ambitions in sustainable design. Few projects will encompass the conditions to meet them all, but the case studies demonstrate their relevance. Separately and together they convey the extensive potentials of 'sustainability in the round' as denoting far more than 'low e building design', important though that is.

Lesson 8
Articulation

Comparatively, the United Kingdom offers many workplace buildings that provide a good standard of accommodation. However, the evolution of this building stock has been strongly led by speculative development, and its design influenced by commercial imperatives that target efficiency, simplicity and cost. Essentially this leads to serviced boxes, with the approach depending on 'bolt on' elements to signal differentiation, rather than integrated design. This approach works well enough to produce buildings designed to provide shelter and safety, but for buildings that reach further it is unlikely to suffice. In providing enriched user experience, articulation can be useful, though it risks seeming gratuitous if not appropriately conceived. The case studies offer instructive references to skilled articulation that is well integrated with the overall design.

The sculpted, compacted forms of the Mersey Valley Processing Centre, and the chimneys and circular terminals of Abbey Mills Pumping Station, are key in defining these buildings as objects of rich visual interest and symbolic expression that communicates externally. So does the articulated ovoid form of the Café on the Square at Brindleyplace, with its strongly profiled echo in the building's butterfly roof. The Jerwood Vanbrugh Theatre is enriched by internal articulation, with the cleft as a faceted cascade around which all the building's spaces and facilities pivot. The cleft's nuanced nature, affording glimpses, visual cues and private moments in window seats, is inextricably linked to its articulated design. North Greenwich Station is the place it is because its articulated design provides legibility, interest and meaning to passengers in what could easily have been a space of oppressive subterranean anomie.

The exciting three-dimensional spatial patchwork of The Third Space derives a palpable buzz from the articulation of the structural elements that originated in the former building on the site. At Citigroup, the articulation of the massive structural cross-braces works to 'hold' one in the tall atrium, providing a reassuring sense of containment without obscuring the wonderful panoramic views out at every level. Inside the atrium, the view to the internal elevations that step in and out of the graduated floor plates and the secondary atria, with the external cladding wrapping round these elevations too, 'explains' the building with its unusual arrangement based on its offset core. At Issey Miyake, the folding in of the external elevation to create the base of the store windows and internal window seats plays to the project objective of dissolving the barrier between the exterior and interior. At the Oxo Tower Restaurant, the single gesture of sloping the front glazed elevation outward says something about being in the sky, as well as facilitating a marvellous and expansive spatial experience. The articulated aerofoil ceiling is a strong exemplar of the fact that the ceiling plane – typically the largest uninterrupted surface that people see inside buildings – can be a source of interest and beauty in itself.

Lesson 9
Spatial quality: volume, scale and proportion

If architecture is the enclosure of space and light, the aim – in exceeding the functions of delivering shelter and safety – is spatial quality. This is essentially delight from being in the space.

The case studies offer examples of wonderful spatial quality, an outcome of many key decisions relating to volume, scale and proportion, to light and its modulation. The Gibbs Building and Wessex Water excel in this, with the rich thoughtfulness of their respective designs and thoroughness of integration. The spatial arrangement in both these buildings plays a key part in the quality of user experience that has been achieved. No part feels too large or small for comfort, too isolated or exposed, or second rate compared to any other part. At 90 m, the floor plates at the Gibbs Building could have felt very linear, and post-occupancy research shows that users dislike long runs of office space that engender a mechanistic sense of workers being placed in serried ranks. Instead, the interplay of vertical elements with the floor plate – the cores that face the atrium and the double-height sub-atria on the Euston Road elevation – has modulated the space. From all the floors, the connection to the atrium volume gives a sense of expansiveness, and the modulation of light through the fritting and white blinds contributes further. The Wessex Water achievement is also about humane scale – in all parts of the building – and the effective transmission and modulation of light through all its wings.

Chiswick Park shows the potential for achieving good spatial quality with a deep plan of some 18 m from core to perimeter glazing. It demonstrates the point that spatial quality derives from an interaction of design decisions involving depth, core design and location, clear height and cladding. The efficient core arrangements, high ceilings and clear views out have created buildings that feel good in all parts of their floor plates.

The fine spatial quality at Issey Miyake, the Oxo Tower Restaurant, the West Reservoir Centre and the City of Manchester Stadium hinges on two high-level principles. The interface between the interior and exterior space enlivens the interior of these buildings with natural light and the spirit of the external space they address, and the proportions are comfortable. Even in the enormous space encompassed by the City of Manchester Stadium, the proportions of the overall building as one looks across the pitch, and the elements that define the way the space on the stands is both delimited and outwardly connected, achieve a result that feels 'right'.

The spatial experience in the atrium at EMI is very much about proportion, light and connection. Whilst a contemporary commercial project would almost inevitably squeeze an atrium down from these proportions – 21.0 m by 10.5 and five storeys high – its plan to sectional dimensions are highly instructive for generating space that feels good. Other design elements also contribute: the angled glazed roof, the cuts through the internal elevations that give meaning to the atrium as a volume as well as in plan, and the reflective white glazed tiling that facilitates the dissemination of natural light in the space.

The Jerwood Vanbrugh Theatre extends the discussion away from spatial quality as an end in itself, 'because it feels good', to further performance characteristics of proportion in plan and section. The formula applied to the relative proportions of the audience seating area and the stage, and their intersection in the volume, has created space that feels intimate and engaging to viewers, and significantly larger to the student performers than it actually is, encouraging them to develop their skill in projection. The detailed case study makes it clear that the theatre's proportions are the fulcrum of this achievement. As in all successful realisations, it is aided by contributory design decisions, such as the replacement of solid balcony fronts with yacht wire, to shift the horizon outward to the theatre walls.

Lesson 10

Spatial sequencing and narrative

Space of equivalently good quality is not necessarily space of equivalent character. Spatial variety contributes to making buildings places of learning, surprise and delight. The Oxo Tower Restaurant receives patrons in a relatively confined space after they exit from the lift core, then leads them through the narrow space along the south-facing elevation into the large open restaurant space. One's sense of discovery and excitement is heightened by the contrast between journey and arrival. The Third Space takes one from its opaque exterior into a reception area that signals promise and drama before one reaches the sequence of spaces in the club itself. Their varying character, associated with the respective activities that each space offers, emanates into the club as a whole. This result fulfils the aim of the brief for the space to reveal the range of activities offered by the club, nudging members to extend their participation.

The route from the new Jerwood Vanbrugh Theatre building to RADA's original building behind it involves a switch in axis, evoking the intricacy in RADA's overall suite of facilities, whilst signalling the way with a clarity that is reassuring. The building's cleft plays a key role in bringing the building's public and academy spaces into a single frame of reference, providing a unifying narrative of the functions that the building serves. At Wessex Water, the progression, as one advances through the building from the entrance involves a spatial sequence that indicates which functions are accommodated. It also suggests the hierarchy of use and 'entitlement' associated with the respective spaces, from the taller, wider street with its shared activities for use by the whole organisation, to the smaller, more intimate wings that serve as bases for the operational teams.

At both Ercol and Nexus, the scope to see all the participants at work on their respective activities, and the clear views to the support facilities – the restaurants and, at Nexus, the computer suite – give narrative meaning to the respective enterprises. The scope to 'read', comprehend and feel part of the range of activities undertaken, and to enjoy the drama of the scale involved, is facilitated by upper-level viewing galleries in both these buildings.

Lesson 11

Building animation

A building that is a bland box may nevertheless house lively activity. Buildings are not the only trigger of social animation, but they have distinctive potentials to animate users' experience of their space. The Citigroup building does this in spades. With its vertical circulation accommodated in the building's offset core, people cross the atrium to reach the main floor plates. Every person's movement around and across the void changes the composition. The reflective stone floor surfaces, in combination with the lighting above, further animate the space, as does the enormous artwork suspended down one elevation.

At Issey Miyake, animation is similarly integral to the design, with the colour on the white walls varying subtly as the external light conditions alter through the day and in relation to the orientation of the vertical planes. The backdrop formed by the marmarino walls sets off the fashion displays, among which the movements of staff and customers appear as visual echoes of the bodily forms that inspire the garments. The large sculptural luminaire contributes another dimension, as its suspended petals flutter with the motion of the fan inside the installation's main cylinder, and as their moving shadows play on the walls. Given the extent to which the store's immediate external setting is visually incorporated in one's experience of the interior, the outside movement of vehicles and people adds another layer to the stimuli within the space.

Lesson 12

Atria and streets that live

Atria and internal streets provide special opportunities to enliven buildings. The converse is also the case: looking down on an inactive atrium base connotes a building as a dead place, and looking up to sealed elevations around an atrium volume or to open elevations that show little sign of activity seems pointless and is dispiriting.

The exemplars illustrate the conditions of atria and streets that live. At Citigroup the atrium is a necessary space to walk round and across in order to use the building. The escalators at its base carry people to the first two floors, ensuring vitality at the lower reaches, despite the closure, on security grounds, of the public passage across the atrium base that the design allows for. EMI's atrium base is the building's heart. Accommodating the catering and informal seating, this is a place that occupants need to use. Its vitality and beauty as light-filled space inspire one to use it. The views down from above show lively usage; the views up encompass the projecting balconies with people moving horizontally along them, the cuts through the elevations to the workspace activity beyond, and the vertical movements of the exposed lifts.

At Wessex Water, the internal street is a key route and also a node. One must use this route to reach the workspace, and it accommodates the building's main shared facilities that are provided in the open plan – the café, informal meeting space and library. It also carries the traffic to the restaurant and meeting rooms. The Gibbs Building's atrium represents all the conditions described. It is 'a place', it accommodates a variety of attractive informal facilities at its base, and it is the building's unique locale for such facilities. It is also the main route to the conference facilities and the building's vertical circulation. Its elevations are extensively open to the workspace on the floors above and to the restaurant on the top floor of the lower block. The ground floor is linked to the reception on the northern side; southward it incorporates the Gower Place entrance and the views to the street beyond. These atria are places that thrum with life.

Lesson 13

Mixed use as a design agenda

Mixed use offers important potential benefits: facilitating people in meeting diverse needs at close range, affording reasons for different constituencies of people to 'be there', and at varying times of day and night, with the resultant vitality that this brings. Mixed use also offers environmental benefits, such as more intensive use of infrastructure and the inherent scope for energy transfer. Historic resistance to mixed use has been on numerous grounds, including discrete building regulations, tenure systems and a preference to manage homogenous categories of user. The recent cultural preference for mixed use requires design strategies to support it.

The paradigmatic case study to illustrate the potential for mixed use is The Mailbox. This is a single building, incorporating 100,000 sq m of accommodation. The range of uses it incorporates is highly diverse – residential, hotel, department store, retail, offices, broadcast transmission, restaurants and bars. The fact that these are provided for within one continuous structure demonstrates the fact that mixed use is 'do-able'; it is feasible to have residents frying chips in the same building from which the BBC broadcasts live television. Indeed, an attraction for the broadcaster to come to this building was the visibility to the public that this lively location would confer, making the organisation more accessible to its licence-payers. In their disposition of the various uses on the extensive Mailbox site, the architects have exploited its contrasting conditions with optimum effect.

The City of Manchester Stadium demonstrates that mixed use can be necessary to achieve a building's financial viability. Its provision is integral to the design and sustenance of this high-quality stadium building. The mix of functions accommodated within the structure is germane to the business model – the conference facilities and sponsors' private dining that support the revenue stream, shopping and catering for the crowds of spectators, changing, physiotherapy and relaxation for the players, offices for the administrative staff, in addition to the essential stands and pitch.

The Oxo Tower project shows the detailed design work needed to facilitate effective co-existence between diverse users in an occupied building. Rather than side-step the real scope for conflict between different uses, the architects have paid particular attention to the separation of service cores and to acoustic insulation between the top floor with its restaurant and the residential accommodation below.

Lesson 14
Room for the influence of others and implicit branding
Design for mixed uses brings to the fore the need for responsive design to encompass varied expression. Total design control that prescribes every element and gesture in complex settings is not compatible with people's experience of cities as pluralistic outcomes of many agents.

The case studies show numerous ways that 'making way' for others can add value. The architects of the West Reservoir Centre have focused on celebrating the tower of the former water filtration plant, giving it current meaning and supplementing it with new wings that provide for contemporary functionality, without seeming to compete with or overtake the building's legacy element. This approach, that affords value to users by making historical layers palpable, is also shown at the Oxo Tower, in the design's gentle reworking of the warehouse elevations and restoration of the lantern.

The Mailbox shows an explicit strategy to make way for other influences. The approach enables retailers to involve their own designers in devising fascia displays that project these companies' own identities and give The Mailbox the vitality of an authentic high street, within a framework that ensures the coherence of the main promenade by maintaining the design grid and providing guidance on aspects such as signage. A similar approach is demonstrated in the EMI building, where the designers developed an effective strategy to meet the twin aims of the executives who wanted the interior to look professional and business-like and the staff who wanted it to feel 'un-corporate', affording scope to express the identities and ethos of the occupying groups in their respective spaces.

At Issey Miyake, confidence in the strength of the store's interior look and feel withstands admission of whatever is happening on the outside into users' visual experience within the space. Indeed, this was a design aim, and its actualisation provides an authentic context for the garments on sale in the store. Similarly at Ercol, the refined quality and effective functionality of the space speak for the furniture designed and produced in it. This is the power of design quality as implicit branding. No need for labels, no need to shout.

Lesson 15
Artwork integral with architecture
Building interiors are not cities in themselves, and buildings designed entirely anew lack historic elements to incorporate. The introduction of artwork to enliven interior spaces has an obvious role. Conventional approaches to image display and the use of plasma screens do add visual interest. However, art that is integral to the architecture, rather than 'stuck on', contributes more profoundly, not least because it invites a three-dimensional engagement that offers a dynamic experience as people move around it.

Several of the case studies demonstrate the major contributions made by collaborations with artists in the projects' design. The Bridget Riley installation of linked parallelograms suspended down the height of the Citigroup atrium, and the voluptuous Thomas Heatherwick sculpture positioned at the Gower Street end of the Gibbs Building's atrium, providing interactive stimulus for both people inside the building and for passers-by, are both magnificent examples. The Ingo Maurer light fixture in the Issey Miyake store contributes not only to animation in the space, but, because the barrier between the outside and inside of the store is barely perceptible, it too offers itself to passers-by, as a magnet reinforcing the store's invitation to participation. All these examples highlight the related point made in Lesson 14 about making space for the influence of others.

Another named artistic collaborator in these examples is Charlie Holmes, whose contribution at the West Reservoir Centre is both to the centre's lighting design and to the brass reliefs that celebrate water.

The large-scale petalled uplighters at Nexus, designed by the architects, are artistic objects, responding to the scale and proportion of the space in which they sit. Mimicking the concept without this contextual appreciation and the flair that they exude would produce lifeless and intrusive objects, rather than the elements of majestic beauty that these are.

Lesson 16

Legibility and comfort: assurance, safety, security

Building signage has grown in prominence as a set of elements that need to be procured, and much of this is well designed, but buildings that rely on signage to give users a sense of orientation and direction fail to impart such knowledge intuitively. The challenge of providing implicit orientation is not confined to complex buildings. Even 'boxes' can be lacking in this respect, resorting to compass points or alphanumeric coordinates on signs that advise users of their location on a floor plate.

Evoking a sense of direction as people approach buildings and when they are inside is more than a courtesy. It promotes comfort, security and safety. The litmus test amongst the exemplars is surely North Greenwich Underground Station – tight on space and lacking in both natural light and any external aspect as a reference point. The architects' grasp of people's needs, and their skill in making the space legible through the use of voids, form, rhythmic repetition, reflective glazing, colour and lighting are masterful.

At Stratford Regional Station the design succeeds in building confidence by heightening both the perception and reality of the building as a safe place. Its large glazed front elevation is significant as a beacon, announcing where one should head and showing that the building is safe inside. For passengers moving from a platform to the exit and vice versa, or changing to another set of lines, the design offers a comprehension of the station's arrangement and clarity on where to go. Numerous features contribute to the strong sense of reassurance and comfort. The visually permeable safety barriers as one crosses the pedestrian bridge over the tracks that run through the station at ground level below, the wide stairs with their easy, gentle gradient, and the substantial landings all give users a feeling of command in the space. The open sightlines, good lighting, views out and lack of clutter in the entrance and concourse contribute to the building's legibility and promote confidence in the station as a safe and secure place. And the thermal comfort and effective lighting further support its calm ambience, a space where it feels good to be.

Safety and user comfort were high priorities in the brief for the City of Manchester Stadium. These inform the innovative design of the entry ramps – more spacious turnstiles and the gentle gradient. Innovation in fire strategy was key to the design of the continuous concourses, allowing for both mass evacuation and ease of movement to WCs and refreshment stations – fulfilling the aims of the brief for coherence, clarity and amenity. Within the stands, the spectator experience benefits from visual clarity. From its column-free cable-net roof structure to the recessed treads on the gangways that reduce adjacent handrail heights, the concept and details of the stadium design accord everyone an unimpeded view of the event. The user comfort afforded by the design's protection from low sun angles and prevailing winds, the natural light that suffuses the stands, the effective ventilation and the design's effectiveness in accommodating most seats in the areas most favoured by spectators contributes to the brief objective for an excellent user experience.

At both the Nexus building and EMI, clear comprehension of the building promotes orientation and ease of use. At Nexus, the views from the large operational floors to the upper galleries with their rest facilities, the reciprocal views down, the clear routes passing through the mezzanine structure between the opposing operational floors, and the views through the glazing that encloses the computer room and the glazed meeting pods that one passes on the way, all help to 'explain' this large facility. The large-scale space is dramatic, but its intelligibility affords reassurance in its use and ensures that it is not overwhelming.

At EMI, the openings in the atrium elevations provide views to the working floors, and the horizontal circulation routes that project into and pass through the void, all play a role in conveying the life in the building. One grasps the overall unifying arrangement, despite the fit-out design that accommodates considerable variety in the look and feel of the numerous team areas.

There are many respects in which the Mailbox exemplifies a project's positive contribution to the realm beyond its boundaries. In addition to its role in place-making, the development enhances legibility in its environs through a series of decorative pavement tiles that signal the route to The Mailbox from New Street Station.

Lesson 17
Colour, texture, reflection and lighting

A building's organisation is key, but colour, texture, reflection and lighting are valuable levers in designing buildings that feel good. These are often dealt with as a successive layer in the design process, with the thought involved disassociated from the architecture – undertaken by different participants, an afterthought and sometimes also rushed.

North Greenwich Underground Station, where these elements are so effectively invoked in defining the building interior, exemplifies the relevance of considering them as potentially powerful influences to shape people's overall spatial experience. The rich user experience in the Citigroup atrium derives in part from the effective use of reflective materials and lighting. These enhance spatial depth and generate added vitality on the routes around and across the void. The quality of light on the materials on which it falls affects the perceived depth of space and the depth and appearance of its surfaces. This is wonderfully demonstrated in the sense of mystery created by the lighting at Abbey Mills Pumping Station. At EMI the uplifting sense of light in the atrium is associated with its white elevations. With the smooth texture of their glazed brick, these might have risked presenting a sterile appearance, but for the bricks' marginal variations in orientation that create a subtle dappling in reflection. The fine lines of blue light that run around the atrium add to the verve.

The two large floor plates inside Nexus are modulated by the use of colour, graduated in three large horizontal bands of deep orange to yellow as one's eye moves from front to back across the space. This banding provides an organisational device, orienting people both within a segment of the operation and as part of the whole. Colour is also integrally used in the design of the support facilities, and the whole space is tied together by the artistic lighting trees with their white fabric petalled sails and their uplight that suffuses the interior with a unifying glow, humanising the building's large scale and softening its sense of drama. At Issey Miyake the extensive use of white planes promotes an appreciation of the play of light and shadow, and forms a well-poised backdrop that is stimulating in itself as well as setting off the vibrant colours of the garments on display.

Lesson 18
Detailing

Whereas good design, in the vein of design that is well thought through, is not inherently more expensive, the execution of good detailing typically does cost more. In addition to potential benefits of increased durability over the building's life cycle, the added cost of well-produced detailing should be viewed in the context of the positive difference it may make to users, day in and day out, over a building's life.

With its concept and form, the Café on the Square at Brindleyplace is all about careful detailing. As a miniature of striking visual prominence that is also viewed in the round, the building's quality and appeal would be considerably diminished without this. The developers' recognition of its significance underlies their view that the building provides good value despite its high cost per square metre.

Like the café building, the design of the Gibbs Building is highly integrated, with the structure in full view as one moves around the building and looks up, down and across the atrium. The integration and interior finishes are immaculate – from arrival at the reception desk, in the beautiful waiting areas, past the confident security station and across the fine limestone flooring. Users then move to the wonderfully finished conference rooms, or the lifts with their electronic displays, and up to the office floors with the finely clad cores, or the restaurant with its perfectly fritted glass roof panels and their excellently fitting blinds. The building oozes quality and confidence. The linked benefit to the Wellcome Trust is the ethos implied by this visual standard – what you see is who they are.

The detailing at Chiswick Park plays a powerful role in defining the development's identity. The finely crafted castings in the external steel frames that support the fixed brise-soleil and the signature external fire stairs comprise a distinctive architectural vocabulary that places Chiswick Park in a quality league. The project's approach to design and construction procurement, based on off-site manufacture followed by building assembly on site, is advantageous in the economies of scale that can be realised for elements such as the castings, when these are replicated following their design's perfection.

The finishes in the case study station buildings are exposed to intensive wear as well as to visual scrutiny. In both North Greenwich, with the artificially illuminated focus on its finishes in the building's confined space, and Stratford with its wide views to surfaces that are bathed in daylight, the detailing is in sharp focus. In both, the refinement of the detailing and its quality of execution make not only for durability, but for passengers' implicit confidence in the facilities' safety and the accountability of the operator. Similar principles apply across all building types. The apparent quality reflects on the values, and by implication the brands, of the building occupiers. The point has particular relevance in infrastructure buildings that are used or seen by the public. Here the physical setting is suggestive of operational standards and the operator's self-confidence, sense of command and respect for the public as users. The approach is well exemplified by the Mersey Valley Processing Centre, where the nature and quality of the external envelope engender confidence in the operation's transparency and accountability.

Lesson 19
Lean *and* rich

Buildings that feel good are poised to inspire, uplift, delight, hold and reassure. These are benefits beyond mere shelter and safety, important as those are. With the recent interest in environmental sustainability, mostly focusing on low energy buildings, professional attention has been addressed at design for technical performance. This concentrates on integrated design and engineering by predominantly passive means, to achieve thermal and lighting conditions that are effective for users. Achieving it is relevant to creating buildings that feel good, not least because sustainable living reflects the values of users just as it does of designers, and research shows considerable user interest in, and support for, 'energy-friendly' accommodation. Further, to the extent that low e building design offers users control of internal environmental conditions (assuming mechanisms can be identified for a level of individual control that avoids conflicts over the control sought by others in close proximity), this represents further progress in producing buildings that feel good. These aims are valid and important, but they are insufficient.

The case studies show that greater value to users can be given at the same time, if sustainably designed buildings are also beautiful. The Gibbs Building and Wessex Water both incorporate a comprehensive repertoire of design measures to lower their environmental impacts. Both also provide interior space of considerable beauty; they excel in demonstrating the more stretching aim. Sustainability goes hand in glove with leanness, but lean buildings can also be rich. The Mersey Valley Processing Centre is spare, whilst placing a rich composition in its Widnes Valley setting. The Manchester City Stadium is lean, whilst offering an enriching asset to the East Manchester skyline, and an exhilarating experience within. The very efficient masterplan for Chiswick Park makes for highly sustainable use of the site, whilst delivering an unusually high level of user amenity and a strong aesthetic identity.

Lesson 20
Aesthetic commitment: it matters despite the metrics

The exemplars underscore the relevance of aesthetic aims to every brief, as a central concern in producing buildings that feel good. These are not aims that are validated according to headcount or square metres. The Mersey Valley Processing Centre and the Abbey Mills Pumping Station are the more valuable as exemplars because aesthetic commitment features so largely in their conception and delivery, despite the fact that hardly anyone works at either building and few people visit them. The Café on the Square at Brindleyplace is a key reference on good briefing because aethetics are central to its vision and execution, in spite of – and to some extent because of – its tiny scale. Aesthetics play a vital role in people's experience of building use.

PRODUCING BUILDINGS THAT FEEL GOOD:
AIDE MÉMOIRE

Hopefully the case studies and the lessons derived from them succeed in establishing a systematic framework to help in designing buildings that feel good. Dissecting the instructive exemplars poses an agenda for action that this chapter frames as a series of questions for project teams to help produce buildings that feel good. Considered at the briefing stage when projects are first conceived, and at subsequent milestones during design evolution, they can serve as an aide mémoire in helping to set, stretch and reassert the potential visions that design proposals can achieve.

The individual case studies, their synthesis in the preceding analysis and their distillation in the suite of questions that follow can be referenced as a repertoire of possible approaches in establishing project aims, guiding their translation into design, and providing a touchstone in design review. Looking forward, and to continuous learning from structured analysis of completed projects, these questions can also be used to inform systematic study of buildings in use – post-occupancy evaluation.

1 Does the project offer scope to contribute to its setting?

2 Is the building's response to its context sensitive and respectful?

3 Is there a role for this building to harness form in helping to make, or re-make, a place?

4 Does the project offer potential as a link in social memory, whilst providing for contemporary functionality with contemporary design?

5 Is there a positive role that can be played by incorporating the building's external realm into users' experience in the interior?

6 Does the design make the most of its potential for natural light (and the play of shadow), and incorporate passive strategies to manage solar gain and excessive brightness?

7 Does the project have a rounded vision for sustainable design that includes social and economic objectives, and are the proposed solutions well integrated?

8 Does articulation have a role in making this building more than a box?

9 Does this project benefit from a conscious focus on producing spatial quality, and are the relevant aspects considered in interrelation – plan, height, volume, scale, proportion, core and envelope?

10 Does the design offer a sequence in spatial experience, and does the spatial arrangement have a role to play in revealing a narrative?

11 Does the design exploit the possibilities for a dynamic experience of the building – through people's engagement with its component spaces and with one another, and in the interplay of space, light and the building's finishes?

12 Has an atrium been modelled to facilitate a pleasing quality of light and transmit it effectively to the adjacent spaces? And do its arrangement, proportions and elevations work to make sense – of its base as a place, and of its volume as an opportunity for effective visual connection to the spaces beyond it?

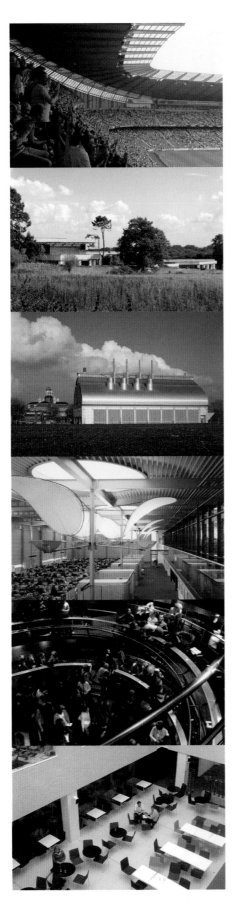

13 Mixed use is a design agenda. Does it have a place within this project's vision, and what can the design do to support its effective operation in use?

14 Does the approach encompass enough self-confident reserve neither to 'shout' nor to monopolise visual expression? Does it allow scope for other relevant influences to impinge in contributing to a rich plurality of user experience, such as integrated historical elements, contemporary artworks or retailers' storefronts? Does the design facilitate or compete with the mission of the activity inside?

15 Is there scope on this project for an integral artistic contribution that will add to people's experience of the space in a continuously engaging way, and without prescribing and dominating their use of the space with 'one single big idea'?

16 Is the project conceived for people who will use the building in varying roles and capacities to feel well-oriented and secure, without it being so predictable and anodyne as to lack continual interest and a sense of exploration?

17 What may colour, materials, lighting and reflections contribute, and how are they interacting in combination, to make users feel good – in THIS space?

18 Based on a long view encompassing the building's projected life, is the detailing designed to a standard that will do it justice over time, and is the responsibility for its execution appropriately vested?

19 Low energy buildings can also be beautiful. Is the focus too exclusively on technical performance at the expense of ambition for the building also to look and feel good?

20 Does the approach to this building incorporate a commitment to it feeling good, even if it is 'only' small, or 'just for' a function with 'low added value', or for accommodation that few people will ever inhabit?

DESIGNING BUILDINGS THAT FEEL GOOD: BECAUSE IT'S WORTH IT

The propositions put forward here are not innovative. Rather, they provide an agenda to which almost every colleague I have ever worked with aspires. The challenges that project teams typically confront are finding the language, framing the questions, and making the project space to set and sustain a vision. These difficulties are heightened by the pressures of programme and by busy professionals' lack of time for thoughtful reflection. Whatever the barriers, this book can be used to introduce the agenda, assert the relevance of people's needs in setting project visions, and reassert them in the evolution of a building's design. It offers a series of pointers that can be adopted without the need to first find a productivity rationale, because most people in the industry want to contribute to the design of buildings that feel good, and because this is do-able once the agenda is set and shared.

If these feature in one's ambitions, the aims that the book defines are worthwhile in their own right. The exemplars' approaches, strategies and solutions provide a rich repertoire of evidence demonstrating that *the achievement of these aims hinges first and foremost on them being set*, then asking the design to meet them. Their realisation is always about thought, commitment and skill, and not always about budget. Of course, the case studies show that talent is useful too.

This book has been written to help people further their own inclinations to design and produce buildings that feel good. It can be used as a framework for project meetings, to inspire and encourage reserved clients, cajole and persuade sceptical colleagues, and as a hand on the shoulder to oneself. Hopefully it will help in facilitating the design of buildings that realise more of what they are inherently able to offer.

Index

Picture credits

Pentland Lakeside
p88 © Nick Wood www.nickwoodphoto.com
pp90–1 All images GHM Rock Townsend
p92 Top and bottom right © Nick Wood
www.nickwoodphoto.com,
bottom left © ZZA Responsive User
Environments
p93 Top © Nick Wood
www.nickwoodphoto.com,
bottom © ZZA Responsive User
Environments

Stratford Regional Station
p94 Dennis Gilbert / VIEW
pp96–7 All images Wilkinson Eyre
p98 Top © Timothy Soar
www.timothysoar.co.uk,
bottom © ZZA Responsive User
Environments
p99 Top left © ImageCapture /
Photography by Joe D Miles
www.joedmiles.com,
top right, bottom left and right © ZZA
Responsive User Environments

The Third Space
p100 © Chris Smailes
p102 Collcutt & Hamp
p103 Top © ImageCapture / Photography
by Joe D Miles www.joedmiles.com,
bottom © ZZA Responsive User
Environments
p104 © Chris Smailes
p105 Both images James Fletcher © Third
Space

Wellcome Trust, Gibbs Building
p106 © ZZA Responsive User Environments
p108 Top left © Wellcome Trust, top right
and bottom Hopkins Architects Ltd
p109 © ZZA Responsive User Environments
p110 © Nick Guttridge / VIEW
p111 Top left © Wellcome Trust,
top middle © ZZA Responsive User
Environments,
top right © Wellcome Trust,
bottom © Nick Kane

Wessex Water
p112 © Peter Cook / Bennetts Associates
p114 Both images Bennetts Associates
p115 Left and bottom right © Peter Cook /
Bennetts Associates,
top right © Richard Frewer
p116 © Peter Cook / VIEW
p117 © Peter Cook / Bennetts Associates

West Reservoir Centre, Stoke Newington
p118 © Marcus Robinson
www.marcusrobinsonphotography.com
p120 Both images Marks Barfield Architects
p121 Both images © Marcus Robinson
www.marcusrobinsonphotography.com
p122 Both images ZZA Responsive User
Environments © CABE
p123 © Marcus Robinson
www.marcusrobinsonphotography.com

Buildings that feel good: lessons for design
*Some thumbnail images are repeated from the
case studies –*
p124 © ZZA Responsive User Environments
p127 Top © ZZA Responsive User
Environments,
bottom © Dennis Gilbert / VIEW
www.dennisgilbert.com
p128 Top © Timothy Soar
www.timothysoar.co.uk,
bottom © Chris Gascoigne / VIEW
p129 © Nick Wood www.nickwoodphoto.com
p130 James Fletcher © Third Space
p131 © Peter Cook / VIEW
p132 © Peter Cook / VIEW
p133 © Peter Cook / Bennetts Associates
p134 Top © Mark Tupper
www.marktupper.co.uk,
bottom © Nick Wood
www.nickwoodphoto.com
p135 Top © Chris Gascoigne, bottom
© Birmingham Development Company
p136 Top © Marcus Robinson
www.marcusrobinsonphotography.com,
bottom © ZZA Responsive User
Environments
p137 © Roderick Coyne – SMC Alsop

p138 © Peter Cook / VIEW
p139 © Brindleyplace
p140 Top © Dennis Gilbert / VIEW,
bottom © Ian Lawson

**Producing buildings that feel good:
aide mémoire**
pp142–3 *Some thumbnail images are repeated
from the case studies –*
from the top to bottom: © ZZA Responsive
User Environments, © Dennis Gilbert /
VIEW www.dennisgilbert.com,
© Timothy Soar www.timothysoar.co.uk,
© Peter Cook / VIEW, James Fletcher
© Third Space, © Brindleyplace,
© Dennis Gilbert / VIEW, © Peter Cook /
Bennetts Associates, © Peter Cook /
VIEW, © Peter Cook / VIEW,
© Brian Avery, © ZZA Responsive
User Environments

**Designing buildings that feel good:
because it's worth it**
p144 *Some thumbnail images are repeated
from the case studies –*
from left to right, top to bottom:
© Nick Wood
www.nickwoodphoto.com,
© Roderick Coyne – SMC Alsop,
© ZZA Responsive User Environments,
© Peter Cook / VIEW, James Fletcher
© Third Space, © Nick Guttridge / VIEW,
© Birmingham Development Company,
© Marcus Robinson
www.marcusrobinsonphotography.com,
© Peter Cook / VIEW,
© ZZA Responsive User
Environments, © Ian Lawson,
© Nick Wood www.nickwoodphoto.com